Containers in OpenStack

Leverage OpenStack services to make the most of Docker,
Kubernetes and Mesos

Pradeep Kumar Singh

Madhuri Kumari

BIRMINGHAM - MUMBAI

Containers in OpenStack

First published: December 2017

Production reference: 1191217

Published by Packt Publishing Ltd.
Livery Place
35 Livery Street
Birmingham
B3 2PB, UK.
ISBN 978-1-78839-438-3

www.packtpub.com

Credits

Authors
Pradeep Kumar Singh
Madhuri Kumari

Reviewers
Felipe Monteiro
Venkatesh Loganathan
Vinoth Kumar Selvaraj

Commissioning Editor
Gebin George

Acquisition Editor
Namrata Patil

Content Development Editor
Amrita Noronha

Technical Editor
Akash Patel

Copy Editor
Safis Editing

Project Coordinator
Shweta H Birwatkar

Proofreader
Safis Editing

Indexer
Francy Puthiry

Graphics
Tania Dutta

Production Coordinator
Shantanu Zagade

About the Authors

Pradeep Kumar Singh is an OpenStack developer. He has expertise in the domains of containers, storage, and web application development. Pradeep is a core reviewer for OpenStack Zun. Pradeep also loves machine learning and the infrastructure part of it. In his free time, he plays with his Raspberry Pi 3 clusters, and also loves to write code in different programming languages.

Madhuri Kumari is an OpenStack developer. She has expertise in the domains of cloud computing, containers, and virtualization. She has been working on OpenStack since December 2014 and is a core reviewer for two OpenStack projects, Magnum and Zun. Besides this, she has also worked on the Ironic, Swift, Murano, and Valence. She is an active speaker at OpenStack summits, LinuxCon, and local meetups. She was also nominated for the RedHat Women in Open Source Award, 2017.

About the Reviewers

Felipe Monteiro currently works for AT&T as a software developer, predominantly focusing on developing AT&T's under-cloud platform (UCP) for orchestrating OpenStack on Kubernetes deployment. He is currently the lead developer for Deckhand and Armada, two of the core microservices that comprise UCP. He also works on OpenStack, particularly on Murano, OpenStack's application catalog, and Patrole, a Tempest plugin responsible for validating the correct implementation of RBAC and API compliance with RBAC. He was the Murano PTL during the Pike release cycle and is currently a core reviewer for both Murano and Patrole.

Venkatesh Loganathan is a senior DevOps engineer at CD Cloudenablers Pvt. Ltd., a product-based cloud technology start up in Chennai, India. He has spent an equal amount of time focusing on release engineering in the agile methodology, automating daily activities through configuration management tools, and maintaining the site at high availability.

> *I would like to thank my Amma, Appa, Anna, and my friends for their love and support. My special thanks to our Cloudenablers team for giving me this opportunity and motivation to explore new technologies.*

Vinoth Kumar Selvaraj is a passionate computer science engineer from Tamil Nadu, India. He works as a DevOps engineer at Cloudenablers Inc.

As an active moderator on Ask OpenStack, he consistently answers and provides solutions for questions posted on the Ask OpenStack forum. Based on karma points, he was ranked 20 out of 20,000 members in the Ask OpenStack forum. He has also written many OpenStack-related articles for `http://superuser.openstack.org/` and hosts a dedicated website for his works on OpenStack at `http://www.hellovinoth.com/`.

You can visit his LinkedIn page at `https://www.linkedin.com/in/vinothkumarselvaraj/` and tweet him `@vinoth6664`.

Vinoth has also authored a book entitled *OpenStack Bootcamp* for Packt.

www.PacktPub.com

For support files and downloads related to your book, please visit `www.PacktPub.com`. Did you know that Packt offers eBook versions of every book published, with PDF and ePub files available? You can upgrade to the eBook version at `www.PacktPub.com` and as a print book customer, you are entitled to a discount on the eBook copy. Get in touch with us at `service@packtpub.com` for more details. At `www.PacktPub.com`, you can also read a collection of free technical articles, sign up for a range of free newsletters and receive exclusive discounts and offers on Packt books and eBooks.

`https://www.packtpub.com/mapt`

Get the most in-demand software skills with Mapt. Mapt gives you full access to all Packt books and video courses, as well as industry-leading tools to help you plan your personal development and advance your career.

Why subscribe?

- Fully searchable across every book published by Packt
- Copy and paste, print, and bookmark content
- On demand and accessible via a web browser

Customer Feedback

Thanks for purchasing this Packt book. At Packt, quality is at the heart of our editorial process. To help us improve, please leave us an honest review on this book's Amazon page at `https://www.amazon.com/dp/1788394380`.

If you'd like to join our team of regular reviewers, you can email us at `customerreviews@packtpub.com`. We award our regular reviewers with free eBooks and videos in exchange for their valuable feedback. Help us be relentless in improving our products

Table of Contents

Preface

Containers are one of the most talked about technologies of recent times. They have become increasingly popular as they are changing the way we develop, deploy, and run software applications. OpenStack gets tremendous traction as it is used by many organizations across the globe and as containers gain popularity and become more complex, it's necessary for OpenStack to provide various infrastructure resources for containers such as compute, network, and storage.

Containerization in OpenStack aims at answering the question, how can OpenStack keep pace with the increasing challenges of container technology? You will start with getting familiar with container and OpenStack basics so that you understand how the container ecosystem and OpenStack work together. To help you get better at compute, networking, managing application services and deployment tools, the book has dedicated chapters for different OpenStack projects: Magnum, Zun, Kuryr, Murano, and Kolla.

Toward the end, you will be introduced to some best practices to secure your containers and COE on OpenStack with an overview of using each OpenStack project for different use cases.

What this book covers

Chapter 1, *Working with Containers*, starts with discussing the history of virtualization and then talks about the evolution of containers. After this, it focuses on explaining containers, their types, and the different container runtime tools. It then dives into Docker and its installation, and also shows how to use Docker to perform operations on containers.

Chapter 2, *Working with Container Orchestration Engines,* starts with an introduction to Container Orchestration Engines and then it introduces different COEs available today. It explains the installation of Kubernetes and how to use it to manage containers in an example application.

Chapter 3, *OpenStack Architecture*, starts with an introduction to OpenStack and its architecture. Then it briefly explains OpenStack's core components and their architecture.

Chapter 4, *Containerization in OpenStack*, explains the need for containerization in OpenStack, and also talks about different OpenStack container-related projects.

Chapter 5, *Magnum – COE Management in OpenStack*, explains the Magnum project of OpenStack in detail. It talks about the concepts, components, and architecture of Magnum. Then, it demonstrates Magnum installation with DevStack and it's hands-on.

Chapter 6, *Zun – Container Management in OpenStack*, explains the Zun project of OpenStack in detail. It talks about the concepts, components, architecture of Zun. Then, it demonstrates Zun installation with DevStack and it's hands-on.

Chapter 7, *Kuryr – Container Plugin for OpenStack Networking*, explains the Kuryr project of OpenStack in detail. It talks about the concepts, components, and architecture of Kuryr. Then, it demonstrates Kuryr installation with DevStack and it's hands-on.

Chapter 8, *Murano – Containerized Application Deployment on OpenStack*, explains the Murano project of OpenStack in detail. It talks about the concepts, components, and architecture of Murano. Then, it demonstrates Murano installation with DevStack and it's hands-on.

Chapter 9, *Kolla – Containerized Deployment of OpenStack*, explains the Kolla project of OpenStack in detail. It talks about the sub-projects, key features and architecture of Kolla. Then, it explains the deployment process for OpenStack ecosystem using the Kolla project.

Chapter 10, *Best Practices for Containers and OpenStack*, summarizes different container-related OpenStack projects and their advantages. Then, it also explains the security issues with containers and the best practices to resolve them.

What you need for this book

This book assumes a basic level of understanding of cloud computing, the Linux operating system and containers. The book will guide you through the installation of any tools that are required.

You can use any tool for the test environment, such as Vagrant, Oracle's VirtualBox, or a VMware workstation.

In this book, the following software list is required:

- Operating system: Ubuntu 16.04
- OpenStack: Pike release or newer
- VirtualBox 4.5 or newer
- Vagrant 1.7 or newer

To run the OpenStack installation in a development environment, the following minimum hardware resources are required:

- A host machine with CPU hardware virtualization support
- 8 core CPU
- 12 GB RAM
- 60 GB free disk space

Internet connectivity is required to download the necessary packages for OpenStack and other tools.

Who this book is for

The book is targeted toward cloud engineers, system administrators, or anyone from the production team who works on the OpenStack cloud. This book acts as an end-to-end guide for anyone who wants to start using the concept of containerization in OpenStack.

Conventions

In this book, you will find a number of styles of text that distinguish between different kinds of information. Here are some examples of these styles, and an explanation of their meaning.

Code words in text, database table names, folder names, filenames, file extensions, pathnames, dummy URLs, user input, and Twitter handles are shown as follows: "The `zun-compute` service is the main component of the Zun system."

Any command-line input or output is written as follows:

```
$ sudo mkdir -p /opt/stack
```

New terms and **important words** are shown in bold. Words that you see on the screen, in menus or dialog boxes for example, appear in the text like this: "You can see in the following screenshot that we are given two options to choose for our container host: **Kubernetes Pod** and **Docker Standalone Host**."

Warnings or important notes appear in a box like this.

 Tips and tricks appear like this.

Reader feedback

Feedback from our readers is always welcome. Let us know what you think about this book-what you liked or disliked. Reader feedback is important for us as it helps us develop titles that you will really get the most out of. To send us general feedback, simply e-mail feedback@packtpub.com, and mention the book's title in the subject of your message. If there is a topic that you have expertise in and you are interested in either writing or contributing to a book, see our author guide at www.packtpub.com/authors.

Customer support

Now that you are the proud owner of a Packt book, we have a number of things to help you to get the most from your purchase.

Downloading the example code

You can download the example code files for this book from your account at http://www.packtpub.com. If you purchased this book elsewhere, you can visit http://www.packtpub.com/support and register to have the files e-mailed directly to you.

You can download the code files by following these steps:

1. Log in or register to our website using your e-mail address and password.
2. Hover the mouse pointer on the **SUPPORT** tab at the top.
3. Click on **Code Downloads & Errata**.
4. Enter the name of the book in the **Search** box.
5. Select the book for which you're looking to download the code files.
6. Choose from the drop-down menu where you purchased this book from.
7. Click on **Code Download**.

Once the file is downloaded, please make sure that you unzip or extract the folder using the latest version of:

- WinRAR / 7-Zip for Windows
- Zipeg / iZip / UnRarX for Mac
- 7-Zip / PeaZip for Linux

The code bundle for the book is also hosted on GitHub at `https://github.com/PacktPublishing/Containers-in-OpenStack`. We also have other code bundles from our rich catalog of books and videos available at `https://github.com/PacktPublishing/`. Check them out!

Errata

Although we have taken every care to ensure the accuracy of our content, mistakes do happen. If you find a mistake in one of our books-maybe a mistake in the text or the code we would be grateful if you could report this to us. By doing so, you can save other readers from frustration and help us improve subsequent versions of this book. If you find any errata, please report them by visiting `http://www.packtpub.com/submit-errata`, selecting your book, clicking on the **Errata Submission Form** link, and entering the details of your errata. Once your errata are verified, your submission will be accepted and the errata will be uploaded to our website or added to any list of existing errata under the Errata section of that title.

To view the previously submitted errata, go to `https://www.packtpub.com/books/content/support` and enter the name of the book in the search field. The required information will appear under the **Errata** section.

Piracy

Piracy of copyrighted material on the Internet is an ongoing problem across all media. At Packt, we take the protection of our copyright and licenses very seriously. If you come across any illegal copies of our works in any form on the Internet, please provide us with the location address or website name immediately so that we can pursue a remedy.

Please contact us at copyright@packtpub.com with a link to the suspected pirated material.

We appreciate your help in protecting our authors and our ability to bring you valuable content.

Questions

If you have a problem with any aspect of this book, you can contact us at questions@packtpub.com, and we will do our best to address the problem.

1
Working with Containers

This chapter covers containers and various topics related to them. In this chapter, we will be covering the following topics:

- The historical context of virtualization
- Introduction to containers
- Container components
- Types of containers
- Types of container runtime tools
- Installation of Docker
- Docker hands-on

The historical context of virtualization

Traditional virtualization appeared on the Linux kernel in the form of hypervisors such as Xen and KVM. This allowed users to isolate their runtime environment in the form of **virtual machines** (**VMs**). Virtual machines run their own operating system kernel. Users attempted to use the resources on host machines as much as possible. However, high densities were difficult to achieve with this form of virtualization, especially when a deployed application was small in size compared to a kernel; most of the host's memory was consumed by multiple copies of kernels running on it. Hence, in such high-density workloads, machines were divided using technologies such as *chroot jails* which provided imperfect workload isolation and carried security implications.

In 2001, an operating system virtualization in the form of Linux vServer was introduced as a series of kernel patches.

This led to an early form of container virtualization. In such forms of virtualization, the kernel groups and isolates processes belonging to different tenants, each sharing the same kernel.

Here is a table that explains the various developments that took place to enable operating system virtualization:

Year and Development	Description
1979: chroot	The concept of containers emerged way back in 1979 with UNIX chroot. Later, in 1982, this was incorporated into BSD. With chroot, users can change the root directory for any running process and its children, separating it from the main OS and directory.
2000: FreeBSD Jails	FreeBSD Jails was introduced by Derrick T. Woolworth at R&D associates in 2000 for FreeBSD. It is an operating system's system call similar to chroot, with additional process sandboxing features for isolating the filesystem, users, networking, and so on.
2001: Linux vServer	Another jail mechanism that can securely partition resources on a computer system (filesystem, CPU time, network addresses, and memory).
2004: Solaris containers	Solaris containers were introduced for x86 and SPARC systems, and first released publicly in February 2004. They are a combination of system resource controls and the boundary separations provided by zones.
2005: OpenVZ	OvenVZ is similar to Solaris containers and makes use of a patched Linux kernel for providing virtualization, isolation, resource management, and checkpointing.
2006: Process containers	Process containers were implemented at Google in 2006 for limiting, accounting, and isolating the resource usage (CPU, memory, disk I/O, network, and so on) of a collection of processes.
2007: Control groups	Control groups, also known as CGroups, were implemented by Google and added to the Linux Kernel in 2007. CGroups help in the limiting, accounting, and isolation of resource usages (memory, CPU, disks, network, and so on) for a collection of processes.
2008: LXC	LXC stands for Linux containers and was implemented using CGroups and Linux namespaces. In comparison to other container technologies, LXC works on the vanilla Linux kernel.

2011: Warden	Warden was implemented by Cloud Foundry in 2011 using LXC at the initial stage; later on, it was replaced with their own implementation.
2013: LMCTFY	**LMCTFY** stands for **Let Me Contain That For You**. It is the open source version of Google's container stack, which provides Linux application containers.
2013: Docker	Docker was started in the year of 2016. Today it is the most widely used container management tool.
2014: Rocket	Rocket is another container runtime tool from CoreOS. It emerged to address security vulnerabilities in early versions of Docker. Rocket is another possibility or choice to use instead of Docker, with the most resolved security, composability, speed, and production requirements.
2016: Windows containers	Microsoft added container support (Windows containers) to the Microsoft Windows Server operating system in 2015 for Windows-based applications. With the help of this implementation, Docker would be able to run Docker containers on Windows natively without having to run a virtual machine to run.

Introduction to containers

Linux containers are operating system level virtualization which provides multiple isolated environments on a single host. Rather than using dedicated guest OS like VMs, they share the host OS kernel and hardware.

Before containers came into the limelight, multitasking and traditional hypervisor-based virtualization were used, mainly. Multitasking allows multiple applications to run on the same host machine, however, it provides less isolation between different applications.

Traditional hypervisor-based virtualization allows multiple guest machines to run on top of host machines. Each of these guest machines runs their own operating system. This approach provides the highest level of isolation as well as the ability to run different operating systems simultaneously on the same hardware.

However, it comes with a number of disadvantages:

- Each operating system takes a while to boot
- Each kernel takes up its own memory and CPU, so the overhead of virtualization is large
- The I/O is less efficient as it has to pass through different layers
- Resource allocation is not done on a fine-grained basis, for example, memory is allocated to a virtual machine at the time of creation, and memory left idle by one virtual machine can't be used by others
- The maintenance load of keeping each kernel up to date is large

The following figure explains the concept of virtualization:

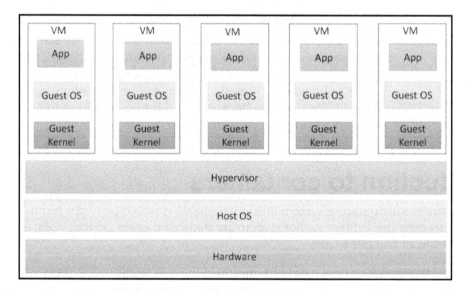

Containers provide the best of both words. To provide an isolated and secure environment for containers, they use Linux kernel features such as chroot, namespaces, CGroups, AppArmor, SELinux profiles, and so on.

The secure access to the host machine kernel from the container is ensured by Linux security modules.. Boot is faster as there is no kernel or operating system to start up. Resource allocation is fine-grained and handled by the host kernel, allowing the effective per container quality of service (QoS). The next figure explains container virtualization.

However, there are some disadvantages of containers compared to traditional hypervisor-based virtualization: guest operating systems are limited to those which can use the same kernel.

Traditional hypervisors provide additional isolation that is not available in containers, meaning the noisy neighbor problem is more significant in containers than it is with a traditional hypervisor:

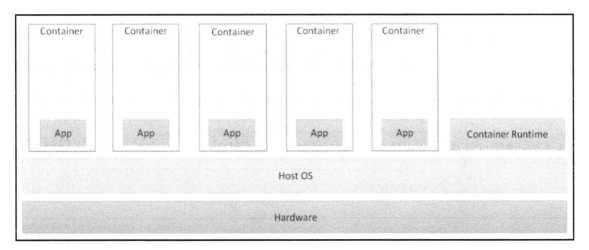

Container components

Linux containers are typically comprised of five major components:

- **Kernel namespaces**: Namespaces are the major building blocks of Linux containers. They isolate various types of Linux resources such as the network, processes, users, and the filesystem into different groups. This allows different groups of processes to have completely independent views of their resources. Other resources that can be segregated include the process ID space, the IPC space, and semaphore space.
- **Control groups**: Control groups, also known as CGroups, limit and account for different types of resource usage such as the CPU, memory, disk I/O, network I/O, and so on, across a group of different processes. They help in preventing one container from resource starvation or contention caused by another container, and thereby maintains QoS.

- **Security**: Security in containers is provided via the following components:
  - **Root capabilities**: This will help in enforcing namespaces in so-called privileged containers by reducing the power of root, in some cases to no power at all.
  - **Discretionary Access Control (DAC)**: It mediates access to resources based on user-applied policies so that individual containers can't interfere with each other and can be run by non-root users securely.
  - **Mandatory Access Controls (MAC)**: Mandatory Access Controls (MAC), such as AppArmor and SELinux, are not required for creating containers, but are often a key element to their security. MAC ensures that neither the container code itself nor the code running in the containers has a greater degree of access than the process itself requires. This way, it minimizes the privileges granted to rogue or compromised processes.
  - **Toolsets**: Above the host kernel lies the user-space toolsets such as LXD, Docker, and other libraries, which help in managing containers:

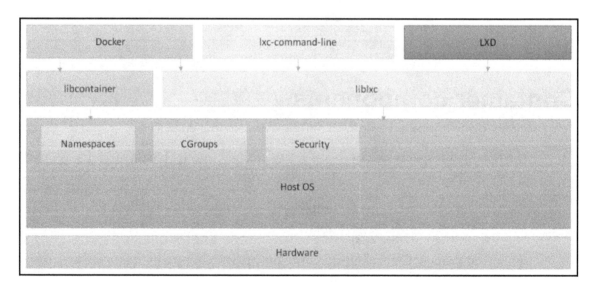

Types of containers

The types of containers are as follows:

Machine containers

Machine containers are virtual environments that share the kernel of the host operating system but provide user space isolation. They look far more similar to virtual machines. They have their own init process, and may run a limited number of daemons. Programs can be installed, configured, and run just as they would be on any guest operating system. Similar to a virtual machine, anything running inside a container can only see resources that have been assigned to that container. Machine containers are useful when the use case is to run a fleet of identical or different flavors of distros.

Machine containers having their own operating system does not mean that they are running a full-blown copy of their own kernel. Rather, they run a few lightweight daemons and have a number of necessary files to provide a separate OS within another OS.

Container technologies such as LXC, OpenVZ, Linux vServer, BSD Jails, and Solaris zones are all suitable for creating machine containers.

The following figure shows the machine container concept:

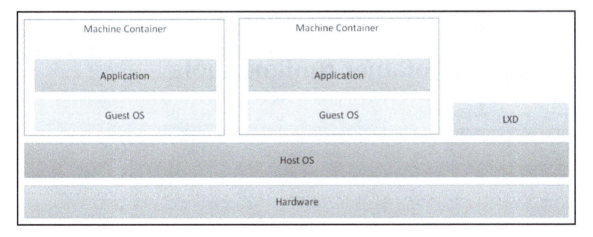

Application containers

While machine containers are designed to run multiple processes and applications, application containers are designed to package and run a single application. They are designed to be very small. They need not contain a shell or `init` process. The disk space required for an application container is very small. Container technologies such as Docker and Rocket are examples of application containers.

The following figure elaborates on application containers:

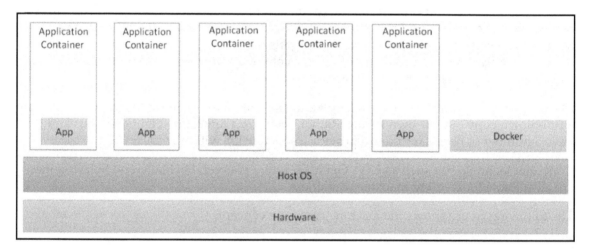

Types of container runtime tools

Multiple solutions are available today for managing containers. This section discusses alternative types of containers.

Docker

Docker is the world's leading container platform software. It has been available since 2013. Docker is a container runtime tool designed to make it easier to create, deploy, and run applications by using containers. Docker has drastically reduced the complexity of managing applications by containerizing them. It allows applications to use the same Linux kernel as the host OS, unlike VMs, which create a whole new OS with dedicated hardware. Docker containers can run both on Linux and Windows workloads. Docker containers have enabled huge efficiencies in the development of software, but require runtime tools such as Swarm or Kubernetes.

Rocket

Rocket is another container runtime tool from CoreOS. It emerged to address security vulnerabilities in early versions of Docker. Rocket is another possibility or choice to Docker, with the most resolved security, composability, speed, and production requirements. Rocket has built things differently to Docker in many aspects. The main difference is that Docker runs a central daemon with root privileges and spins off a new container as its sub process, whereas Rocket never spins a container with root privileges. However, Docker always recommends running containers within SELinux or AppArmor. Since then, Docker has come up with many solutions to tackle the flaws.

LXD

LXD is a container hypervisor for managing LXC by Ubuntu. LXD is a daemon which provides a REST API for running containers and managing related resources. LXD containers provide the same user experience as traditional VMs, but using LXC, which provides similar runtime performance to containers and improved utilization over VMs. LXD containers run a full Linux OS so are typically long running, whereas Docker application containers are short-lived. This makes LXD a machine management tool that is different to Docker and is closer to software distribution.

OpenVZ

OpenVZ is a container-based virtualization for Linux which allows the running of multiple secure, isolated Linux containers also known as **virtual environments** (**VEs**) and **virtual private server** (**VPS**) on a single physical server. OpenVZ enables better server utilization and ensures that applications do not conflict. It is similar to LXC. It can only run on a Linux-based OS. Since all OpenVZ containers share the same kernel version as hosts, users are not allowed to do any kernel modification. However, it also has the advantage of a low memory footprint due to the shared host kernel.

Windows Server containers

Windows Server 2016 introduced Linux containers to Microsoft workloads. Microsoft has partnered with Docker to bring the benefits of the Docker container to Microsoft Windows Server. They have also re-engineered the core windows OS to enable container technology. There are two types of Windows containers: Windows server containers and Hyper-V isolation.

Windows server containers are used for running application containers on Microsoft workloads. They use process and namespace isolation technology for ensuring the isolation between multiple containers. They also share the same kernel as the host OS, as these containers require the same kernel version and configuration as the host. These containers do not provide a strict security boundary and should not be used to isolate untrusted code.

Hyper-V containers

Hyper-V containers are types of Windows containers which provide higher security compared to Windows server containers. Hyper-V hosts Windows server containers in lightweight, highly optimized **Hyper-V** virtual machines. Thus, they bring a higher degree of resource isolation, but at the cost of efficiency and density on the host. They can be used when the trust boundaries of the host OS requires additional security. In this configuration, the kernel of the container host is not shared with other containers on the same host. Since these containers do not share the kernel with the host or other containers on the host, they can run kernels with different versions and configurations. Users can choose to run containers with or without Hyper-V isolation at runtime.

Clear container

Virtual machines are secure but very expensive and slow to start, whereas containers are fast and provide a more efficient alternative, but are less secure. Intel's Clear containers are a trade-off solution between hypervisor-based VMs and Linux containers that offer agility similar to that of conventional Linux containers, while also offering the hardware-enforced workload isolation of hypervisor-based VMs.

A Clear container is a container wrapped in its own individual ultra-fast, trimmed down VM which offers security and efficiency. The Clear container model uses a fast and lightweight QEMU hypervisor that has been optimized to reduce memory footprints and improve startup performance. It has also optimized, in the kernel, the systemd and core user space for minimal memory consumption. These features improve the resource utilization efficiency significantly and offer enhanced security and speed compared to traditional VMs.

Intel Clear containers provide a lightweight mechanism to isolate the guest environment from the host and also provide hardware-based enforcement for workload isolation. Moreover, the OS layer is shared transparently and securely from the host into the address space of each Intel Clear container, providing an optimal combination of high security with low overhead.

With the security and agility enhancements offered by Clear containers, they have seen a high adoption rate. Today, they seamlessly integrate with the Docker project with the added protection of Intel VT. Intel and CoreOS have collaborated closely to incorporate Clear containers into CoreOS's Rocket (Rkt) container runtime.

Installation of Docker

Docker is available in two editions, **Community Edition (CE)** and **Enterprise Edition (EE)**:

- **Docker Community Edition (CE)**: It is ideal for developers and small teams looking to get started with Docker and may be experimenting with container-based apps
- **Docker Enterprise Edition (EE)**: It is designed for enterprise development and IT teams who build, ship, and run business critical applications in production at scale

This section will demonstrate the instructions for installing Docker CE on Ubuntu 16.04. The Docker installation package, available in the official Ubuntu 16.04 repository, may not be the latest version. To get the latest and greatest version, install Docker from the official Docker repository. This section shows you how to do just that:

1. First, add the GPG key for the official Docker repository to the system:

```
$ curl -fsSL https://download.docker.com/linux/ubuntu/gpg |
sudo apt-key add
```

2. Add the Docker repository to APT sources:

```
$ sudo add-apt-repository "deb [arch=amd64]
https://download.docker.com/linux/ubuntu $(lsb_release -cs) stable"
```

3. Next, update the package database with the Docker packages from the newly added repository:

```
$ sudo apt-get update
```

4. Make sure you are about to install Docker repository instead of the default Ubuntu 16.04 repository:

```
$ apt-cache policy docker-ce
```

5. You should see an output similar to the following:

```
docker-ce:
  Installed: (none)
  Candidate: 17.06.0~ce-0~ubuntu
  Version table:
     17.06.0~ce-0~ubuntu 500
        500 https://download.docker.com/linux/ubuntu xenial/stable
        amd64 Packages
     17.03.2~ce-0~ubuntu-xenial 500
        500 https://download.docker.com/linux/ubuntu xenial/stable
        amd64 Packages
     17.03.1~ce-0~ubuntu-xenial 500
        500 https://download.docker.com/linux/ubuntu xenial/stable
        amd64 Packages
     17.03.0~ce-0~ubuntu-xenial 500
        500 https://download.docker.com/linux/ubuntu xenial/stable
        amd64 Packages
```

Notice that `docker-ce` is not installed, but the candidate for installation is from the Docker repository for Ubuntu 16.04. The `docker-ce` version number might be different.

6. Finally, install Docker:

```
$ sudo apt-get install -y docker-ce
```

7. Docker should now be installed, the daemon started, and the process enabled to start on boot. Check that it's running:

```
$ sudo systemctl status docker
docker.service - Docker Application Container Engine
   Loaded: loaded (/lib/systemd/system/docker.service; enabled;
vendor preset: enabled)
   Active: active (running) since Sun 2017-08-13 07:29:14 UTC; 45s
ago
     Docs: https://docs.docker.com
 Main PID: 13080 (dockerd)
   CGroup: /system.slice/docker.service
           ├─13080 /usr/bin/dockerd -H fd://
           └─13085 docker-containerd -l
   unix:///var/run/docker/libcontainerd/docker-containerd.sock --
   metrics-interval=0 --start
```

8. Verify that Docker CE is installed correctly by running the hello-world image:

```
$ sudo docker run hello-world
Unable to find image 'hello-world:latest' locally
latest: Pulling from library/hello-world
b04784fba78d: Pull complete
Digest:
sha256:f3b3b28a45160805bb16542c9531888519430e9e6d6ffc09d72261b0d26
ff74f
Status: Downloaded newer image for hello-world:latest

Hello from Docker!
This message shows that your installation appears to be
working correctly.
```

```
To generate this message, Docker took the following steps:
The Docker client contacted the Docker daemon
The Docker daemon pulled the hello-world image from the Docker Hub
The Docker daemon created a new container from that image,
which ran the executable that produced the output you are
currently reading
The Docker daemon streamed that output to the Docker client,
which sent it to your terminal
To try something more ambitious, you can run an Ubuntu
container with the following:
 $ docker run -it ubuntu bash
Share images, automate workflows, and more with a free Docker ID:
https://cloud.docker.com/
For more examples and ideas,
visit: https://docs.docker.com/engine/userguide/.
```

Docker hands-on

This section explains how to use Docker to run any application inside containers. The Docker installation explained in the previous section also installs the docker command-line utility or the Docker client. Let's explore the `docker` command. Using the `docker` command consists of passing it a chain of options and commands followed by arguments.

The syntax takes this form:

```
$ docker [option] [command] [arguments]
# To see help for individual command
$ docker help [command]
```

To view system wide information about Docker and the Docker version, use the following:

```
$ sudo docker info
$ sudo docker version
```

Docker has many subcommands to manage multiple resources managed by the Docker daemon. Here is a list of management commands supported by Docker:

Management command	Description
Config	Manages Docker configs
container	Manages containers
image	Manages images
network	Manages networks
Node	Manages Swarrn nodes
Plugin	Manages plugins
secret	Manages Docker secrets
Service	Manages services
Stack	Manages Docker stacks
Swarm	Manages swarm
System	Manages Docker
Volume	Manages volumes

In the next section, we will explore container and image resources.

Working with Docker images

An image is a lightweight, standalone executable package that includes everything needed to run a piece of software, including the code, a runtime, libraries, environment variables, and configuration files. Docker images are used to create Docker containers. Images are stored in the Docker Hub.

Listing images

You can list all of the images that are available in the Docker host by running the Docker images subcommand. The default Docker images will show all top-level images, their repository and tags, and their size:

```
$ sudo docker images
REPOSITORY          TAG             IMAGE ID            CREATED
SIZE
wordpress           latest          c4260b289fc7        10 days ago
406MB
mysql               latest          c73c7527c03a        2 weeks ago
412MB
hello-world         latest          1815c82652c0        2 months ago
1.84kB
```

Getting new images

Docker will automatically download any image that is not present in the Docker host system. The `docker pull` subcommand will always download the image that has the latest tag in that repository if a tag is not provided. If a tag is provided, it pulls the specific image with that tag.

To pull a base image, do the following:

```
$ sudo docker pull Ubuntu
# To pull specific version
$ sudo docker pull ubuntu:16.04
```

Searching Docker images

One of the most important features of Docker is that a lot of people have created Docker images for a variety of purposes. Many of these have been uploaded to Docker Hub. You can easily search for Docker images in the Docker Hub registry by using the docker search subcommand:

```
$ sudo docker search ubuntu
NAME                                                DESCRIPTION
STARS       OFFICIAL    AUTOMATED
rastasheep/ubuntu-sshd                              Dockerized SSH service,
built on top of of...   97                          [OK]
ubuntu-upstart                                      Upstart is an event-based
replacement for ...   76          [OK]
ubuntu-debootstrap                                  debootstrap --
```

```
variant=minbase --components...   30           [OK]
nuagebec/ubuntu                                Simple always updated Ubuntu
docker images...   22             [OK]
tutum/ubuntu                                   Simple Ubuntu docker images
with SSH access    18
```

Deleting images

To delete an image, run the following:

```
$ sudo docker rmi hello-world
Untagged: hello-world:latest
Untagged: hello-
world@sha256:b2ba691d8aac9e5ac3644c0788e3d3823f9e97f757f01d2ddc6eb5458df9d8
01
Deleted:
sha256:05a3bd381fc2470695a35f230afefd7bf978b566253199c4ae5cc96fafa29b37
Deleted:
sha256:3a36971a9f14df69f90891bf24dc2b9ed9c2d20959b624eab41bbf126272a023
```

Please refer to the Docker documentation for the rest of the commands related to Docker images.

Working with Docker containers

A container is a runtime instance of an image. It runs completely isolated from the host environment by default, only accessing host files and ports if configured to do so.

Creating containers

Launching a container is simple, as docker run passes the image name you would like to run and the command to run this within the container. If the image doesn't exist on your local machine, Docker will attempt to fetch it from the public image registry:

```
$ sudo docker run --name hello_world ubuntu /bin/echo hello world
```

In the preceding example, the container will start, print hello world, and then stop. Containers are designed to stop once the command executed within them has exited.

As an example, let's run a container using the latest image in Ubuntu. The combination of the -i and -t switches gives you interactive shell access to the container:

```
$ sudo docker run -it ubuntu
root@a5b3bce6ed1b:/# ls
bin  boot  dev  etc  home  lib  lib64  media  mnt  opt  proc  root
run  sbin  srv  sys  tmp  usr  var
```

Listing containers

You can list the all containers running on the Docker host using the following:

```
# To list active containers
$ sudo docker ps
# To list all containers
$ sudo docker ps -a
CONTAINER ID        IMAGE              COMMAND                      CREATED
STATUS                       PORTS             NAMES
2db72a5a0b99        ubuntu                     "/bin/echo hello w..."
58 seconds ago      Exited (0) 58 seconds ago
hello_world
```

Checking container's logs

You can also view the information logged by a running container using the following:

```
$ sudo docker logs hello_world
hello world
```

Starting containers

You can start a stopped container using the following:

```
$ sudo docker start hello_world
```

Similarly, you can use commands such as stop, pause, unpause, reboot, restart, and so on to operate containers.

Deleting containers

You can also delete a stopped container using the following:

```
$ sudo docker delete hello_world
# To delete a running container, use -force parameter
$ sudo docker delete --force [container]
```

Please refer to the Docker documentation for the rest of the commands related to Docker containers.

Summary

In this chapter, we have learned about containers and their types. We have also learned about the components in containers. We took a look at the different container runtime tools. We took a deep dive into Docker, we installed it, and we did a hands-on exercise. We also learned the commands for managing containers and images using Docker. In the next chapter, we will read about different COE tools available today.

2
Working with Container Orchestration Engines

In this chapter, we will be looking at the **Container Orchestration Engine** (COE). Container Orchestration Engines are tools which help in managing many containers running on multiple hosts.

In this chapter, we will be covering the following topics:

- Introduction to COE
- Docker Swarm
- Apache Mesos
- Kubernetes
- Kubernetes installation
- Kubernetes hands-on

Introduction to COE

Containers provide users with an easy way to package and run their applications. Packaging involves defining the library and tools that are necessary for a user's application to run. These packages, once converted to images, can be used to create and run containers. These containers can be run anywhere, whether it's on developer laptops, QA systems, or production machines, without any change in environment. Docker and other container runtime tools provide the facility to manage the life cycle of such containers.

Using these tools, users can build and manage images, run containers, delete containers, and perform other container life cycle operations. But these tools can only manage one container on a single host. When we deploy our application on multiple containers and multiple hosts, we need some kind of automation tool. This type of automation is generally called orchestration. Orchestration tools provide a number of features, including:

- Provisioning and managing hosts on which containers will run
- Pulling the images from the repository and instantiating the containers
- Managing the life cycle of containers
- Scheduling containers on hosts based on the host's resource availability
- Starting a new container when one dies
- Scaling the containers to match the application's demand
- Providing networking between containers so that they can access each other on different hosts
- Exposing these containers as services so that they can be accessed from outside
- Health monitoring of the containers
- Upgrading the containers

Generally, these kinds of orchestration tools provide declarative configuration in YAML or JSON format. These definitions carry all of the information related to containers including image, networking, storage, scaling, and other things. Orchestration tools use these definitions to apply the same setting to provide the same environment every time.

There are many container orchestration tools available, such as Docker Machine, Docker Compose, Kuberenetes, Docker Swarm, and Apache Mesos, but this chapter focuses only on Docker Swarm, Apache Mesos, and Kubernetes.

Docker Swarm

Docker Swarm is a native orchestration tool from Docker itself. It manages a pool of Docker hosts and turns them into a single virtual Docker host. Docker Swarm provides a standard Docker API to manage containers on the cluster. It's easy for users to move to Docker Swarm if they are already using Docker to manage their containers.

Docker Swarm follows a *swap, plug, and play* principle. This provides pluggable scheduling algorithms, a broad registry, and discovery backend support in the cluster. Users can use various scheduling algorithms and discovery backends as per their needs. The following diagram represents the Docker Swarm architecture:

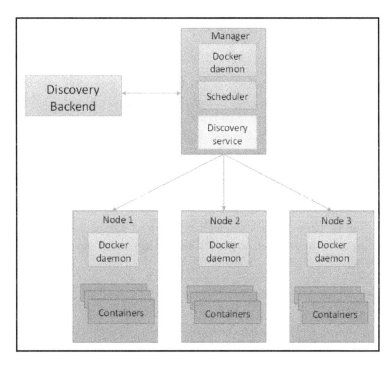

Docker Swarm components

The following sections explain the various components in Docker Swarm.

Node

Node is an instance of the Docker host participating in the Swarm cluster. There can be one or multiple nodes in a single Swarm cluster deployment. Nodes are categorized into Manager and Worker based on their roles in the system.

Manager node

The Swarm manager node manages the nodes in the cluster. It provides the API to manage the nodes and containers across the cluster. Manager nodes distribute units of work, also known as tasks, to worker nodes. If there are multiple manager nodes, then they select a single leader to perform an orchestration task.

Worker node

The worker node receives and executes task distributed by manager nodes. By default, every manager node is also a worker node, but they can be configured to run Manager tasks exclusively. Worker nodes run agents and keep track of tasks running on them, and reports them. The Worker node also notifies the manager node about the current state of assigned tasks.

Tasks

Task is the individual Docker container with a command to run inside the container. The manager assigns the tasks to worker nodes. Tasks are the smallest unit of scheduling in the cluster.

Services

Service is the interface for a set of Docker containers or tasks running across the Swarm cluster.

Discovery service

The Discovery service stores cluster states and provides node and service discoverability. Swarm supports a pluggable backend architecture that supports etcd, Consul, Zookeeper, static files, lists of IPs, and so on, as discovery services.

Scheduler

The Swarm scheduler schedules the tasks on different nodes in the system. Docker Swarm comes with many built-in scheduling strategies that gives users the ability to guide container placement on nodes in order to maximize or minimize the task distribution across the cluster. The random strategy is also supported by Swarm. It chooses a random node to place the task on.

Swarm mode

In version 1.12, Docker introduced the Swarm mode, built into its engine. To run a cluster, the user needs to execute two commands on each Docker host:

To enter Swarm mode:

```
$ docker swarm init
```

To add a node to the cluster:

```
$ docker swarm join
```

Unlike Swarm, Swarm mode comes with service discovery, load balancing, security, rolling updates and scaling, and so on, built into the Docker engine itself. Swarm mode makes the management of the cluster easy since it does not require any orchestration tools to create and manage the cluster.

Apache Mesos

Apache Mesos is an open source, fault-tolerant cluster manager. It manages a set of nodes called slaves and offers their available computing resources to frameworks. Frameworks take the resource availability from the master and launches the tasks on the slaves. Marathon is one such framework, which runs containerized applications on the Mesos cluster. Together, Mesos and Marathon become a container orchestration engine like Swarm or Kubernetes.

The following diagram represents the whole architecture:

Apache Mesos and its components

Here is a list of Apache Mesos components:

Master

Master manages the slave nodes in the system. There may be many masters in the system, but only one is elected as leader.

Slaves

Slaves are the nodes which offer their resources to the master and run the tasks provided by frameworks.

Frameworks

Frameworks are long running applications consisting of schedulers which take resource offers from the master and execute the tasks on the slave.

Offer

Offer is nothing but a collection of each slave node's available resources. The master gets these offers from slave nodes and provides them to frameworks, which in turn runs tasks on the slave nodes

Tasks

Tasks are the smallest unit of work scheduled by frameworks to be run on slave nodes. For example, a containerized application can be one task

Zookeeper

Zookeeper is a centralized configuration manager in a cluster. Mesos uses Zookeeper to elect a master and for slaves to join the cluster

In addition, the Mesos Marathon framework provides service discovery and load balancing for long running applications, such as containers. Marathon also provides the REST API to manage workloads.

Kubernetes

Kubernetes is a container orchestration engine created by Google, designed to automate the deployment, scaling, and operating of containerized applications. It is one of the fastest developing COEs because it provides a reliable platform to build distributed applications on a massive scale. Kubernetes automates your application, manages its life cycle, and maintains and tracks resource allocation in a cluster of servers. It can run application containers on physical or virtual machine clusters.

It provides a unified API to deploy web applications, databases, and batch jobs. It comprises of a rich set of complex features:

- Auto-scaling
- Self-healing infrastructure
- Configuration and updating of batch jobs
- Service discovery and load balancing
- Application life cycle management
- Quota management

Kubernetes architecture

This section outlines the Kubernetes architecture and the various components that deliver a running cluster.

Kubernetes consists of the following components from a top-level view:

- External requests
- Master node
- Worker nodes

The following diagram shows the architecture of Kubernetes:

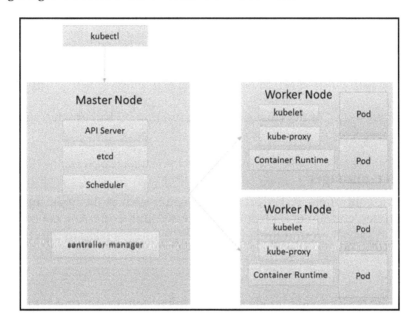

We will discuss each of the components in detail in the next section. Some of the key components are depicted in the diagram.

External request

Users interact with Kubernetes cluster through APIs; they explain what their requirements are and what their application looks like, and Kubernetes does all the hard work to manage their application. `kubectl` is command-line tool from the Kubernetes project to call Kubernetes APIs in a simple way.

Master node

The master node provides the cluster's control plane. It acts like a controller in the cluster. Most of the major functionalities, such as scheduling, service discovery, load balancing, responding to cluster events, and so on, are done by components running on the master node only. Now, let's take a look at the master components and their functionalities.

kube-apiserver

It exposes the Kubernetes APIs. All of the internal and external requests go through the API server. It verifies all of the incoming requests for authenticity and the right level of access, and then forwards the requests to targeted components in the cluster.

etcd

`etcd` is used for storing all of the cluster state information by Kubernetes. `etcd` is a critical component in Kubernetes.

kube-controller-manager

There are multiple controllers in the Kubernetes cluster such as the node controller, replication controller, endpoints controller, service account, and token controllers. These controllers are run as background threads that handle routine tasks in the cluster.

kube-scheduler

It watches all of the newly created pods and schedules them to run on a node if they aren't assigned to any node.

Please read the Kubernetes documentation (`https://kubernetes.io/docs/concepts/overview/components/`) to learn about other components in the control plane, including:

- Cloud-controller-manager
- Web UI
- Container resource monitoring
- Cluster level logging

Worker nodes

The worker nodes run the user's applications and services. There can be one or more worker node in the cluster. You can add or remove nodes from the cluster to achieve scalability in the cluster. Worker nodes also run multiple components to manage applications.

kubelet

`kubelet` is the primary agent that lives on every worker node. It listens to the `kube-apiserver` for commands to perform. Some of the functionalities of `kubelet` include mounting the pod's volume, downloads the pod's secrets, running the pod's containers via Docker or specified container runtime, and so on.

kube-proxy

It enables the service abstraction for Kubernetes by maintaining network rules on the host and performing connection forwarding.

Container runtime

Either Docker or Rocket to create containers.

supervisord

`supervisord` is a lightweight process monitor and control system that can be used to keep `kubelet` and Docker running.

fluentd

`fluentd` is a daemon which helps provide cluster-level logging.

Concepts in Kubernetes

In the following sections, we will learn about the concepts of Kubernetes that are used to represent your cluster.

Pod

A pod is the smallest deployable unit of computing in Kubernetes. A pod is a group of one or more containers with shared storage or a shared network, and a specification of how to run the containers. Containers themselves are not assigned to hosts, whereas closely related containers are always co-located and co-scheduled together as pods and run in a shared context.

A pod models an application-specific logical host; it contains one or more application container, and they are relatively tightly coupled. In a pre-container world, they would have executed on the same physical or virtual machine. Using pods, we have the advantage of better resource sharing, guaranteed fate sharing, inter-process communication and simplified management.

Replica sets and replication controllers

Replica sets are the next generation of replication controllers. The only difference between both is that replica sets support the more advanced set-based selectors whereas replication controllers only support equality-based selectors, therefore making replica sets more flexible than replication controllers. However, the following explanation applies to both.

A pod is ephemeral and won't be rescheduled if the node it is running on goes down. The replica set ensures that a specific number of pod instances (or replicas) are running at any given time.

Deployments

Deployment is high-level abstraction which creates replica sets and pods. Replica sets maintain the desired number of pods in a running state. Deployment provides an easy way to upgrade, rollback, and scale up or scale down pods by just changing the deployment specification.

Secrets

Secrets are used to store sensitive information such as usernames, passwords, OAuth tokens, certificates, and SSH keys. It's safer and more flexible to store such sensitive information in secrets rather than putting them in pod templates. Pods can refer these secrets and use the information inside them.

Labels and selectors

Labels are key value pairs that can be attached to objects, such as pods and even nodes. They are used to specify the identifying attributes of objects that are meaningful and relevant to users. Labels can be attached to objects at creation time and added or modified later. They are used to organize and select subsets of objects. Some examples include environment (development, testing, production, release), stable, pike, and so on.

Labels don't provide uniqueness. Using label selectors, a client or user can identify and subsequently manage a group of objects. This is the core grouping primitive of Kubernetes and it is used in many situations.

Kubernetes supports two kinds of selectors: equality-based and set-based. Equality-based uses key value pairs to filter based on basic equality or inequality, whereas set-based are a bit more powerful and allow for the filtering of keys according to a set of values.

Services

As pods are short-lived objects in Kubernetes, the IP address assigned to them can't be relied upon to be stable for a long time. This makes the communication between pods difficult. Hence, Kubernetes has introduced the concept of a service. A service is an abstraction on top of a number of pods and a policy by which to access them, typically requiring the running of a proxy for other services to communicate with it via a virtual IP address.

Volumes

Volume provides persistent storage to pods or containers. If data is not persisted on external storage, then once the container crashes, all of its files will be lost. Volumes also make data sharing easy between multiple containers inside the pod. Kubernetes supports many types of volumes, and pods can use any number of volumes simultaneously.

Kubernetes installation

Kubernetes can run on various platforms, from laptops and VMs on a cloud provider to a rack of bare metal servers. There are multiple solutions today to install and run Kubernetes clusters. Read the Kubernetes documentation to find the best solution for your particular use case.

In this chapter, we will use `kubeadm` to bring up a Kubernetes cluster on Ubuntu 16.04+. `kubeadm` can be used to easily bring up a cluster with a single command per machine.

In this installation, we will use a tool called kubeadm, which is a part of Kubernetes. The prerequisites for installing kubeadm are:

- One or more machines running Ubuntu 16.04+
- Minimum of 1 GB or more of RAM per machine
- Full network connectivity between all machines in the cluster

All of the machines in the cluster need the following components to be installed:

1. Install Docker on all of the machines. As per the Kubernetes documentation, version 1.12 is recommended. Please refer to the *Installation of Docker* section in Chapter 1, *Working with Containers*, for instructions on installing Docker.

2. Install kubectl on each machine. kubectl is a command-line tool from Kubernetes to deploy and manage applications on Kubernetes. You can use kubectl to inspect cluster resources, create, delete, and update components, and look at your new cluster and bring up example apps. Again, there are multiple options to install kubectl. In this chapter, we will use curl to install it. Please refer to the Kubernetes documentation for more options.

    1. Download the latest release of kubectl using curl:

    ```
    $ curl -LO https://storage.googleapis.com/kubernetes-
    release/release/$(curl -s https://storage.googleapis.com/kubernetes
    release/release/stable.txt)/bin/linux/amd64/kubectl
    ```

    2. Make the kubectl binary executable:

    ```
    $ chmod +x ./kubectl
    ```

3. Now, install kubelet and kubeadm on all the machines. kubelet is the component that runs on all of the machines in your cluster and does things such as starting pods and containers. kubeadm is the command to bootstrap the cluster:

    1. Log in as root:

    ```
    $ sudo -i
    ```

    2. Update and install the packages:

    ```
    $ apt-get update && apt-get install -y apt-transport-https
    ```

3. Add the authenticate key for the package:

```
$ curl -s https://packages.cloud.google.com/apt/doc/apt-key.gpg
| apt-key add -
```

4. Add the Kubernetes source to the apt list:

```
$ cat <<EOF >/etc/apt/sources.list.d/kubernetes.list
deb http://apt.kubernetes.io/ kubernetes-xenial main
EOF
```

5. Update and install the tools:

```
$ apt-get update
$ apt-get install -y kubelet kubeadm
```

The following steps demonstrate how to set up a secure Kubernetes cluster using kubeadm. We will also create a pod network on the cluster so that the application components can talk to each other. Finally, install a sample microservices application on the cluster to verify the installation.

1. Initialize the master node. To initialize the master, choose one of the machines you previously installed kubeadm on and run the following command. We have specified pod-network-cidr for providing the network for communication between pods:

```
$ kubeadm init --pod-network-cidr=10.244.0.0/16
```

Please refer to the kubeadm reference document to read more about the flags kubeadm init provides.

This may take several minutes, as kubeadm init will first run a series of pre-checks to ensure that the machine is ready to run Kubernetes. It might expose warnings and exit on errors depending on the pre-check results. It will then download and install the control plane components and cluster database.

The output of the preceding command looks like this:

```
[kubeadm] WARNING: kubeadm is in beta, please do not use it for
production clusters.
[init] Using Kubernetes version: v1.7.4
[init] Using Authorization modes: [Node RBAC]
[preflight] Running pre-flight checks
[preflight] WARNING: docker version is greater than the most
recently validated version. Docker version: 17.06.1-ce. Max
```

```
validated version: 1.12
[preflight] Starting the kubelet service
[kubeadm] WARNING: starting in 1.8, tokens expire after 24 hours by
default (if you require a non-expiring token use --token-ttl 0)
[certificates] Generated CA certificate and key.
[certificates] Generated API server certificate and key.
[certificates] API Server serving cert is signed for DNS names
[galvin kubernetes kubernetes.default kubernetes.default.svc
kubernetes.default.svc.cluster.local] and IPs [10.96.0.1 10.0.2.15]
[certificates] Generated API server kubelet client certificate and
key.
[certificates] Generated service account token signing key and
public key.
[certificates] Generated front-proxy CA certificate and key.
[certificates] Generated front-proxy client certificate and key.
[certificates] Valid certificates and keys now exist in
"/etc/kubernetes/pki"
[kubeconfig] Wrote KubeConfig file to disk:
"/etc/kubernetes/admin.conf"
[kubeconfig] Wrote KubeConfig file to disk:
"/etc/kubernetes/kubelet.conf"
[kubeconfig] Wrote KubeConfig file to disk:
"/etc/kubernetes/controller-manager.conf"
[kubeconfig] Wrote KubeConfig file to disk:
"/etc/kubernetes/scheduler.conf"
[apiclient] Created API client, waiting for the control plane to
become ready
[apiclient] All control plane components are healthy after
62.001439 seconds
[token] Using token: 07fb67.033bd701ad81236a
[apiconfig] Created RBAC rules
[addons] Applied essential addon: kube-proxy
[addons] Applied essential addon: kube-dns
Your Kubernetes master has initialized successfully:
mkdir -p $HOME/.kube
sudo cp -i /etc/kubernetes/admin.conf $HOME/.kube/config
sudo chown $(id -u):$(id -g) $HOME/.kube/config
You should now deploy a pod network to the cluster.
Run kubectl apply -f [podnetwork].yaml with one of the options
listed at: http://kubernetes.io/docs/admin/addons/.
You can now join any number of machines by running the following on
each node as the root:
kubeadm join --token 07fb67.033bd701ad81236a 10.0.2.15:6443
```

Save the `kubeadm join` command from the preceding output. You will need this to join nodes to your Kubernetes cluster. The token is used for mutual authentication between the master and the nodes.

Now, to start using your cluster, run the following commands as a regular user:

```
$ mkdir -p $HOME/.kube
$ sudo cp -i /etc/kubernetes/admin.conf $HOME/.kube/config
$ sudo chown $(id -u):$(id -g) $HOME/.kube/config
```

2. Install a pod network. This network is used for the communication between pods in the cluster:

> The network must be deployed before running any application. Also, services such as `kube-dns` will not start up before a network is installed. `kubeadm` only supports **Container Network Interface** (**CNI**) networks and does not support `kubenet`.

There are multiple network add-on projects which can be used to create a secure network. To see a complete list, please visit the Kubernetes documentation for reference. In this example, we will use flannel for the networking. Flannel is an overlay network provider:

```
$ sudo kubectl apply -f
https://raw.githubusercontent.com/coreos/flannel/master/Documentati
on/kube-flannel.yml
  serviceaccount "flannel" created
  configmap "kube-flannel-cfg" created
  daemonset "kube-flannel-ds" created
  $ sudo kubectl apply -f
https://raw.githubusercontent.com/coreos/flannel/master/Documentati
on/kube-flannel-rbac.yml
  clusterrole "flannel" created
  clusterrolebinding "flannel" created
```

You can confirm that it is working by checking that the `kube-dns` pod is up and running in the output:

```
$ kubectl get pods --all-namespaces
NAMESPACE       NAME                                 READY     STATUS
RESTARTS    AGE
kube-system     etcd-galvin                          1/1       Running
0           2m
kube-system     kube-apiserver-galvin                1/1       Running
0           2m
kube-system     kube-controller-manager-galvin       1/1       Running
```

```
0           2m
kube-system    kube-dns-2425271678-lz9fp          3/3        Running
0           2m
kube-system    kube-flannel-ds-f9nx8              2/2        Running
2           1m
kube-system    kube-proxy-wcmdg                   1/1        Running
0           2m
kube-system    kube-scheduler-galvin             1/1        Running
0           2m
```

3. Join the nodes to the cluster. To add nodes to the Kubernetes cluster, and SSH to the node and run the following:

```
$ sudo kubeadm join --token <token> <master-ip>:<port>
[kubeadm] WARNING: kubeadm is in beta, please do not use it for
production clusters.
[preflight] Running pre-flight checks
[discovery] Trying to connect to API Server "10.0.2.15:6443"
[discovery] Created cluster-info discovery client, requesting info
from "https://10.0.2.15:6443"
[discovery] Cluster info signature and contents are valid, will use
API Server "https://10.0.2.15:6443"
[discovery] Successfully established connection with API Server
"10.0.2.15:6443"
[bootstrap] Detected server version: v1.7.4
[bootstrap] The server supports the Certificates API
(certificates.k8s.io/v1beta1)
[csr] Created API client to obtain unique certificate for this
node, generating keys and certificate signing request
[csr] Received signed certificate from the API server, generating
KubeConfig...
[kubeconfig] Wrote KubeConfig file to disk:
"/etc/kubernetes/kubelet.conf"
Node join complete:
Certificate signing request sent to master and response
Received
Kubelet informed of new secure connection details
Run kubectl get nodes on the master to see this machine join.
```

Now, run the following command to verify the joining of the nodes:

```
$ kubectl get nodes
NAME        STATUS      AGE         VERSION
brunno      Ready       14m         v1.7.4
```

Verify your installation by creating a sample Nginx pod:

```
$ kubectl run my-nginx --image=nginx --replicas=2 --port=80
deployment "my-nginx" created
$ kubectl get pods
NAME                          READY    STATUS     RESTARTS    AGE
my-nginx-4293833666-c4c5p     1/1      Running    0           22s
my-nginx-4293833666-czrnf     1/1      Running    0           22s
```

Kubernetes hands-on

We learned how to install the Kubernetes cluster in the previous section. Now, let's create a more complex example with Kubernetes. In this application, we will deploy an application running a WordPress site and MySQL database using official Docker images.

1. Create a persistent volume. Both WordPress and MySQL will use this volume to store data. We will create two local persistent volumes of size 5 GB each. Copy the following content to the `volumes.yaml` file:

```
apiVersion: v1
kind: PersistentVolume
metadata:
  name: pv-1
  labels:
    type: local
spec:
  capacity:
    storage: 5Gi
  accessModes:
    - ReadWriteOnce
  hostPath:
    path: /tmp/data/pv-1
   storageClassName: slow
---
apiVersion: v1
kind: PersistentVolume
metadata:
  name: pv-2
  labels:
    type: local
spec:
  capacity:
    storage: 5Gi
  accessModes:
    - ReadWriteOnce
```

```
hostPath:
  path: /tmp/data/pv-2
storageClassName: slow
```

2. Now, create the volume by running the following command:

```
$ kubectl create -f volumes.yaml
persistentvolume "pv-1" created
persistentvolume "pv-2" created
```

3. Check that the volumes were created:

```
$ kubectl get pv
NAME          CAPACITY      ACCESSMODES   RECLAIMPOLICY   STATUS
CLAIM         STORAGECLASS   REASON       AGE
pv-1          5Gi           RWO           Retain          Available
8s
pv-2          5Gi           RWO           Retain          Available
8s
```

4. Create a secret to store the MySQL password. This secret will be referenced by the MySQL and WordPress pods so that those pods will have access to it:

```
$ kubectl create secret generic mysql-pass -from-
literal=password=admin
secret "mysql-pass" created
```

5. Verify that the secrets were created:

```
$ kubectl get secrets
NAME                  TYPE                                      DATA
AGE
default-token-1tb58   kubernetes.io/service-account-token       3
3m
mysql-pass            Opaque                                    1
9s
```

6. Create the MySQL deployment. We will now create a service that exposes a MySQL container, a persistent volume claim of 5 GB, and a deployment running the pod with the MySQL container. Copy the following content to the `mysql-deployment.yaml` file:

```
apiVersion: v1
kind: Service
metadata:
  name: wordpress-mysql
```

```
    labels:
      app: wordpress
spec:
  ports:
    - port: 3306
  selector:
    app: wordpress
    tier: mysql
  clusterIP: None
---
apiVersion: v1
kind: PersistentVolumeClaim
metadata:
  name: mysql-pv-claim
  labels:
    app: wordpress
spec:
  accessModes:
    - ReadWriteOnce
  resources:
    requests:
      storage: 5Gi
  storageClassName: slow
---
apiVersion: extensions/v1beta1
kind: Deployment
metadata:
  name: wordpress-mysql
  labels:
    app: wordpress
spec:
  strategy:
    type: Recreate
  template:
    metadata:
      labels:
        app: wordpress
        tier: mysql
    spec:
      containers:
      - image: mysql:5.6
        name: mysql
        env:
        - name: MYSQL_ROOT_PASSWORD
          valueFrom:
            secretKeyRef:
              name: mysql-pass
              key: password
```

```
          ports:
          - containerPort: 3306
            name: mysql
          volumeMounts:
          - name: mysql-persistent-storage
            mountPath: /var/lib/mysql
        volumes:
        - name: mysql-persistent-storage
          persistentVolumeClaim:
            claimName: mysql-pv-claim
```

7. Now, launch the MySQL pod:

```
$ kubectl create -f mysql-deployment.yaml
service "wordpress-mysql" created
persistentvolumeclaim "mysql-pv-claim" created
deployment "wordpress-mysql" created
```

8. Check the status of the pod:

```
$ kubectl get pods
NAME                                    READY    STATUS    RESTARTS
AGE
  wordpress-mysql-2222028001-18x9x    1/1         Running   0
6m
```

9. Alternatively, you can check the logs of the pod by running the following:

```
$ kubectl logs wordpress-mysql-2222028001-18x9x
Initializing database
2017-08-27 15:30:00 0 [Warning] TIMESTAMP with implicit DEFAULT
value is deprecated. Please use --explicit_defaults_for_timestamp
server
option (see documentation for more details).
2017-08-27 15:30:00 0 [Note] Ignoring --secure-file-priv value as
server is running with --bootstrap.
2017-08-27 15:30:00 0 [Note] /usr/sbin/mysqld (mysqld 5.6.37)
starting as process 36 ...
2017-08-27 15:30:03 0 [Warning] TIMESTAMP with implicit DEFAULT
value is deprecated. Please use --explicit_defaults_for_timestamp
server
option (see documentation for more details).
2017-08-27 15:30:03 0 [Note] Ignoring --secure-file-priv value as
server is running with --bootstrap.
2017-08-27 15:30:03 0 [Note] /usr/sbin/mysqld (mysqld 5.6.37)
starting as process 59 ...
Please remember to set a password for the MySQL root user!
```

```
To do so, start the server, then issue the following
commands:
/usr/bin/mysqladmin -u root password 'new-password'
/usr/bin/mysqladmin -u root -h wordpress-mysql-2917821887-dccql
password 'new-password'
```

Alternatively, you can run the following:

```
/usr/bin/mysql_secure_installation
```

This will also give you the option of removing the test databases and anonymous user created by default. It is strongly recommended for production servers.

Check the manual for more instructions:

Please report any problems at `http://bugs.mysql.com/`.

The latest information about MySQL is available on the web at `http://www.mysql.com`.

Support MySQL by buying support/licenses at: `http://shop.mysql.com`.

Please note that a new default `config` file was not created; please make sure your `config` file is current.

The default `config` file, `/etc/mysql/my.cnf`, exists on the system.

This file will be read by default by the MySQL server. If you do not want to use this, either remove it or use the following command:

```
--defaults-file argument to mysqld_safe when starting the server
Database initialized
MySQL init process in progress...
2017-08-27 15:30:05 0 [Warning] TIMESTAMP with implicit DEFAULT
value is deprecated. Please use --explicit_defaults_for_timestamp
server option (see documentation for more details).
2017-08-27 15:30:05 0 [Note] mysqld (mysqld 5.6.37) starting as
process 87 ...
Warning: Unable to load '/usr/share/zoneinfo/iso3166.tab' as time
zone. Skipping it.
Warning: Unable to load '/usr/share/zoneinfo/leap-seconds.list' as
```

```
time zone. Skipping it.
Warning: Unable to load '/usr/share/zoneinfo/zone.tab' as time
zone. Skipping it.
```

The MySQL `init` process is now done. We are ready for startup:

```
2017-08-27 15:30:11 0 [Warning] TIMESTAMP with implicit DEFAULT
value is deprecated. Please use --explicit_defaults_for_timestamp
server
option (see documentation for more details).
2017-08-27 15:30:11 0 [Note] mysqld (mysqld 5.6.37) starting as
process 5 ...
```

Check the status of persistent volume claims by running the following:

```
$ kubectl get pvc
NAME                STATUS    VOLUME    CAPACITY    ACCESSMODES
STORAGECLASS    AGE
mysql-pv-claim    Bound     pv-1      5Gi         RWO
slow            2h
wp-pv-claim       Bound     pv-2      5Gi         RWO
slow            2h
```

Create the WordPress deployment. We will now create a service that exposes a WordPress container, a persistent volume claim of 5 GB, and a deployment running the pod with the WordPress container. Copy the following content to the `wordpress-deployment.yaml` file:

```yaml
apiVersion: v1
kind: Service
metadata:
  name: wordpress
  labels:
    app: wordpress
spec:
  ports:
    - port: 80
  selector:
    app: wordpress
    tier: frontend
  type: NodePort
---
apiVersion: v1
kind: PersistentVolumeClaim
metadata:
  name: wp-pv-claim
  labels:
```

```
        app: wordpress
spec:
  accessModes:
    - ReadWriteOnce
  resources:
    requests:
      storage: 5Gi
  storageClassName: slow


---
apiVersion: extensions/v1beta1
kind: Deployment
metadata:
  name: wordpress
  labels:
    app: wordpress
spec:
  strategy:
    type: Recreate
  template:
    metadata:
      labels:
        app: wordpress
        tier: frontend
    spec:
      containers:
      - image: wordpress:4.7.3-apache
        name: wordpress
        env:
        - name: WORDPRESS_DB_HOST
          value: wordpress-mysql
        - name: WORDPRESS_DB_PASSWORD
          valueFrom:
            secretKeyRef:
              name: mysql-pass
              key: password
        ports:
        - containerPort: 80
          name: wordpress
        volumeMounts:
        - name: wordpress-persistent-storage
          mountPath: /var/www/html
      volumes:
      - name: wordpress-persistent-storage
        persistentVolumeClaim:
          claimName: wp-pv-claim
```

10. Now, launch the WordPress pod:

```
$ kubectl create -f wordpress-deployment.yaml
service "wordpress" created
persistentvolumeclaim "wp-pv-claim" created
deployment "wordpress" created
```

11. Check the status of the service:

```
$ kubectl get services wordpress
NAME          CLUSTER-IP       EXTERNAL-IP    PORT(S)        AGE
wordpress     10.99.124.161    <nodes>        80:31079/TCP   4m
```

The application is up and running now!

The following lists the commands needed to delete all of the resources created:

- To delete your secret:

```
$ kubectl delete secret mysql-pass
```

- To delete all of the deployments and services:

```
$ kubectl delete deployment -l app=wordpress
$ kubectl delete service -l app=wordpress
```

- To delete the persistent volume claims and the persistent volumes:

```
$ kubectl delete pvc -l app=wordpress
$ kubectl delete pv pv-1 pv-2
```

Summary

In this chapter, we have learned about container orchestration engines. We looked at the different COEs such as Docker Swarm and Apache Mesos. We dealt with Kubernetes and its architecture, components, and concepts in detail.

We learned how to install a Kubernetes cluster using the `kubeadm` tool. Then, at the end, we did a hands-on exercise to run a MySQL WordPress application on a Kubernetes cluster. In the next chapter, we will read about the OpenStack architecture and its core components.

3

OpenStack Architecture

This chapter will start with an introduction to OpenStack. Then this chapter will explain the architecture of OpenStack and further explain each core project in OpenStack. Finally, the chapter will demonstrate DevStack installation and use it for doing some operations with OpenStack. This chapter will cover the following:

- Introduction to OpenStack
- OpenStack architecture
- Introduction to KeyStone, the OpenStack identity service
- Introduction to Nova, the OpenStack compute service
- Introduction to Neutron, the OpenStack network service
- Introduction to Cinder, the OpenStack block storage service
- Introduction to Glance, the OpenStack image service
- Introduction to Swift, the OpenStack object service
- DevStack installation

Introduction to OpenStack

OpenStack is a free and open source software for creating private and public clouds. It provides interrelated sets of components to manage and access large pools of compute, networking and storage resources spanned across a datacenter. Users can manage it either using web-based user interfaces and command lines or REST APIs. OpenStack was open sourced in 2010 by Rackspace and NASA. Currently, it is managed by The OpenStack Foundation, a non-profit entity.

OpenStack architecture

The following figure (from: https://docs.openstack.org/arch-design/design.html)
represents the logical architecture of OpenStack and how users can connect to various
services. OpenStack has multiple components for different purposes such as Nova for
managing compute resources, Glance for managing OS images, and so on. We will learn
about each component in detail in the upcoming sections.

In very simple terms, if a user requests to provision a VM using CLI or the APIs, the request
is handled by Nova. Nova then talks to KeyStone to authenticate the request, Glance for the
OS image, and Neutron for setting up the network resources. Then, after receiving
responses from each component, it boots the VM and returns a response to the user:

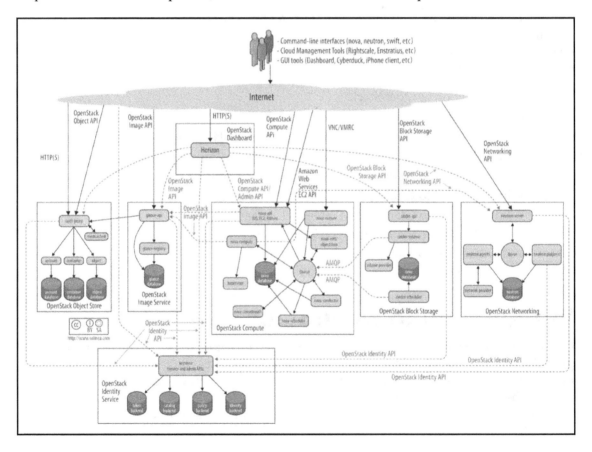

Introduction to KeyStone, the OpenStack identity service

KeyStone is an OpenStack identity service which provides the following capabilities:

- **Identity provider**: In OpenStack, identity is represented as a user in the form of a name and password. In simple setups, KeyStone stores the identity of a user in its database. But it is recommended you use third-party identity providers such as LDAP in production.
- **API client authentication**: Authentication is validating a user's identity. KeyStone can do it by using many third-party backends such as LDAP and AD. Once authenticated, the user gets a token which he/she can use to access other OpenStack service APIs.
- **Multitenant authorization**: KeyStone provides the authorization to access a particular resource by adding a role to every user in every tenant. When a user access any OpenStack service, the service verifies the role of the user and whether he/she can access the resource.
- **Service discovery**: KeyStone manages a service catalog in which other services can register their endpoints. Whenever any other service wants to interact to any particular service, it can refer to the service catalog and can get the address of that service.

KeyStone contains the following components:

- **KeyStoneAPI**: KeyStone API is a WSGI application which handles all the incoming requests
- **Services**: KeyStone is comprised of many internal services exposed over an API endpoint. These services are consumed by a frontend API in a combined fashion
- **Identity**: The identity service handles requests related to user credential validation and CRUD operations associated with users and group data. In production environments, third-party entities such as LDAP can be used as an identity service backend
- **Resource**: The resource service is responsible for managing data related to projects and domains
- **Assignment**: The assignment service is responsible for roles and assigning roles to users
- **Token**: The token service is responsible for managing and validating tokens

- **Catalog**: The catalog service is responsible for managing service endpoints and providing discovery services
- **Policy**: The policy service is responsible for providing rule-based authorization

The following figure represents the architecture of KeyStone:

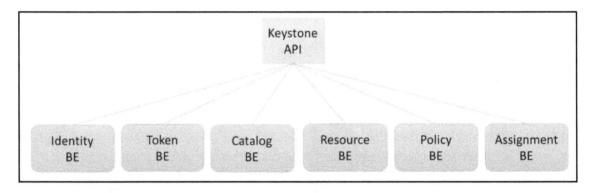

Introduction to Nova, the OpenStack compute service

Nova is a compute service for OpenStack which provides a way to provision compute instances, also known as virtual machines. Nova has capabilities to create and manage the following:

- Virtual machines
- Bare metal servers
- System containers

Nova contains multiple services, each performing different functions. They internally communicate via RPC message-passing mechanisms.

Nova consists of the following components:

- **Nova API**: The Nova API service processes incoming REST requests to create and manage virtual servers. The API service mainly deals with database reads and writes, and communicates over RPC with other services to generate responses to the REST requests.

- **Placement API**: Nova Placement API service was introduced in 14.0.0 Newton release. This service tracks the resource provider inventories and usages of each provider. A resource provider can be a shared storage pool, compute node and so on.
- **Scheduler**: The scheduler service decides which compute host gets instances.
- **Compute**: The compute service is responsible for communicating with hypervisors and virtual machines. It runs on each compute node.
- **Conductor**: The conductor service acts as a database proxy, handles object conversion and helps with request coordination.
- **Database**: The database is an SQL database for data storage.
- **Messaging queue**: This route's information is moved between different Nova services.
- **Network**: The network service manages IP forwarding, bridges, VLANs and so on.

The following figure represents the architecture of Nova:

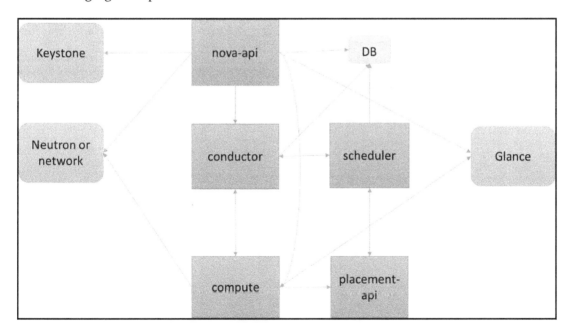

Introduction to Neutron, the OpenStack network service

Neutron is network service for OpenStack which provides a variety of networking options in an OpenStack cloud. Its old name was Quantum and it was later renamed to Neutron. Neutron uses a vast array of plugins to provide different network configurations.

Neutron contains the following components:

- **Neutron server** (neutron-server and neutron-*-plugin): The Neutron server handles incoming REST API requests. It communicates to the database using plugins
- **Plugin agent** (neutron-*-agent): The plugin agent runs on each compute node to manage the local virtual switch (vswitch) configuration
- **DHCP agent** (neutron-dhcp-agent): The DHCP agent provides DHCP services to tenant networks. This agent is responsible for maintaining all DHCP configurations
- **L3 agent** (neutron-l3-agent): The L3 agent provides L3/NAT forwarding for the external network access of VMs on tenant networks
- **Network provider services (SDN server/services)**: This service provides additional networking services to tenant networks
- **Messaging queue**: Routes information between the Neutron processes
- **Database**: The database is an SQL database for data storage

The following figure represents the architecture of Neutron:

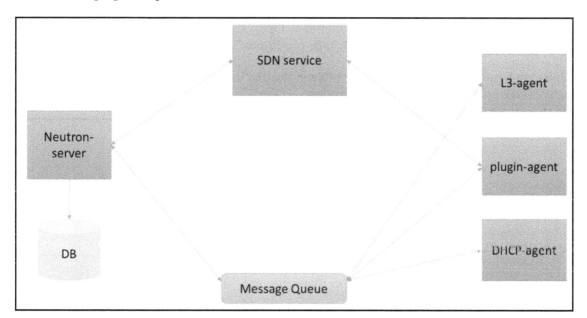

Introduction to Cinder, the OpenStack block storage service

Cinder is a block storage service for OpenStack which provides persistent block storage resources for VMs in Nova. Cinder uses LVM or other plugin drivers to provide storage. Users can use Cinder to create, delete, and attach a volume. Also, more advanced features such as clone, extend volumes, snapshots, and write images can be used as bootable persistent instances for VMs and bare metals. Cinder can also be used independently of other OpenStack services.

The block storage service consists of the following components and provides a highly available, fault tolerant and recoverable solution for managing volumes:

- **cinder-api**: A WSGI app that authenticates and routes requests to the cinder-volume service
- **cinder-scheduler**: Schedules requests for the optimal storage provider node to create volume on

- **cinder-volume**: Interacts with a variety of storage providers and also handles the read and write requests to maintain states. It also interacts with cinder-scheduler
- **cinder-backup**: Backs up volumes to OpenStack object storage (Swift). It also interacts with a variety of storage providers

Messaging queue routes information between the block storage processes. The following figure is the architecture diagram of Cinder:

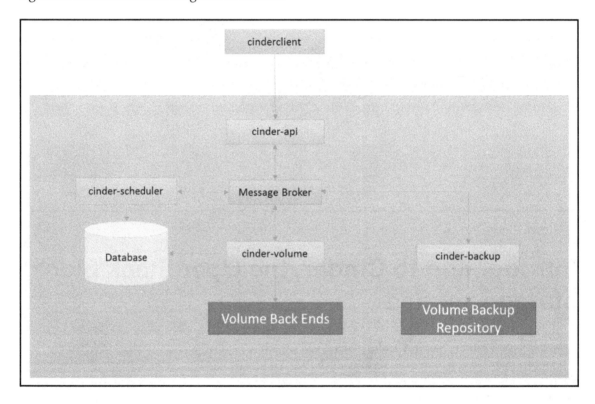

Introduction to Glance, the OpenStack image service

Glance is the image service project for OpenStack which provides discovering, registering, and retrieving abilities for disk and server images. Users can upload and discover data images and metadata definitions that are meant to be used with other services. In short, Glance is a central repository for managing images for VMs, containers and bare metals. Glance has a RESTful API that allows for the querying of image metadata as well as the retrieval of the actual image.

The OpenStack image service, Glance, includes the following components:

- **glance-api**: A WSGI app that accepts image API calls for image discovery, retrieval and storage. It authenticates it with Keystone and forwards the request to the glance-registry.
- **glance-registry**: A private internal service that stores, processes and retrieves metadata about images. Metadata includes items such as size and type.
- **Database**: It stores image metadata. You can choose MySQL or SQLite according to your preferences.
- **Storage repository for image files**: Various repository types are supported for storing images.
- **Metadata definition service**: A common API for vendors, admins, services and users to meaningfully define their own custom metadata. This metadata can be used for different types of resources such as images, artifacts, volumes, flavors and aggregates. A definition includes the new property's key, description, constraints, and the resource type it can be associated with.

The following figure is the architecture diagram of Glance. Glance also has a client-server architecture that provides a REST API to the user, through which requests to the server can be performed:

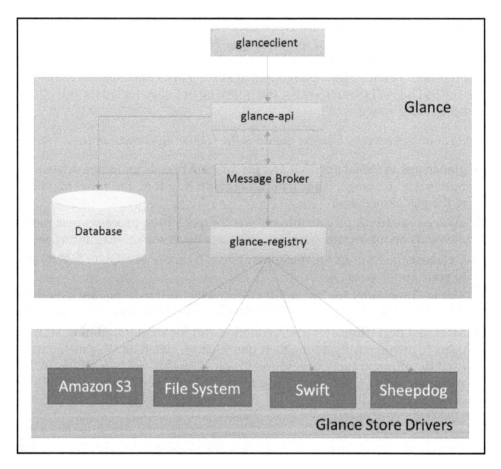

Introduction to Swift, the OpenStack object store

Swift is the object store service for OpenStack which can be used to store redundant, scalable data on clusters of servers that are capable of storing petabytes of data. It provides a fully distributed, API-accessible storage platform that can be integrated directly into applications or used for backup, archiving and data retention. Swift uses a distributed architecture with no central point of control, which makes it highly available, distributed and eventually a consistent object storage solution. It is ideal for storing unstructured data which can grow without bounds and can be retrieved and updated.

Data is written to multiple nodes that extend to different zones for ensuring data replication and integrity across the cluster. Clusters can scale horizontally by adding new nodes. In case of node failure, the data is replicated to other active nodes.

Swift organizes data in a hierarchy. It accounts for the stored list of containers, containers for storing lists of objects and objects for storing the actual data with metadata.

Swift has the following major components in order to deliver high availability, high durability, and high concurrency. Swift has many other services such as updaters, auditors, and replicators which handle housekeeping tasks to deliver a consistent object storage solution:

- **proxy-servers**: The public API is exposed through the proxy server. It handles all of the incoming API requests and routes the request to appropriate services.
- **Rings**: Ring maps the logical names of data to locations on particular disks. There are separate rings for different resources in Swift.
- **Zones**: A zone isolates data from other zones. If a failure happens in one zone, the cluster is not impacted as the data is replicated across zones.
- **Accounts**: An account is a database that stores the list of containers in an account. It is distributed across the cluster.
- **Containers**: A container is a database that stores the list of objects in a container. It is distributed across the cluster.
- **Objects**: The data itself.
- **Partitions**: It stores objects, account databases and container databases and helps manage locations in which data lives in the cluster.

The following figure shows an architecture diagram for Swift:

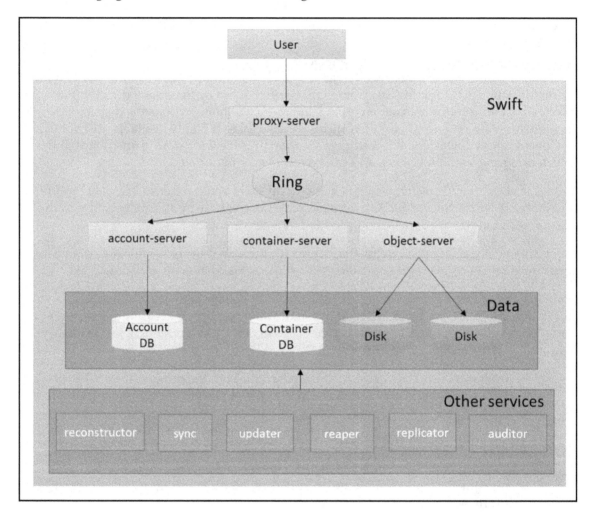

DevStack installation

DevStack is a set of extensible scripts used to quickly bring up a complete development OpenStack environment. DevStack is meant for only development and testing purposes. Please note that it should not be used in a production environment. DevStack installs all the core components by default which are Nova, Neutron, Cinder, Glance, Keystone, and Horizon.

Devstack is able to run on Ubuntu 16.04/17.04, Fedora 24/25, and CentOS/RHEL 7, as well as Debian and OpenSUSE.

In this section, we will set up a basic OpenStack environment on Ubuntu 16.04 and try out some commands to test various components in OpenStack.

1. Add a stack user using the following method. You should run DevStack as a non-root user with `sudo` enabled:

   ```
   $ sudo useradd -s /bin/bash -d /opt/stack -m stack
   ```

2. Now add the `sudo` privilege to the user.

   ```
   $ echo "stack ALL=(ALL) NOPASSWD: ALL" | sudo tee
   /etc/sudoers.d/stack
   $ sudo su - stack
   ```

3. Download DevStack. DevStack by defaults installs the master version of the project from Git. You can specify the use of stable branches also:

   ```
   $ git clone https://git.openstack.org/openstack-dev/devstack
   /opt/stack/devstack
   $ cd /opt/stack/devstack
   ```

4. Create a `local.conf` file. This is a `config` file used by DevStack for installation. Here is the minimum configuration required by DevStack to get started (please refer to `https://docs.openstack.org/devstack/latest/` for more configurations):

   ```
   $ cat > local.conf << END
   [[local|localrc]]
   DATABASE_PASSWORD=password
   RABBIT_PASSWORD=password
   SERVICE_TOKEN=password
   SERVICE_PASSWORD=password
   ADMIN_PASSWORD=password
   enable_service s-proxy
   enable_service s-object
   enable_service s-container
   enable_service s-account
   END
   ```

5. Start the installation. This may take around 15 to 20 minutes depending on your internet connectivity and your host capacity:

   ```
   $ ./stack.sh
   ```

You will see output similar to the following:

```
=========================
DevStack Component Timing
=========================
Total runtime      3033
run_process         24
test_with_retry      3
apt-get-update      19
pip_install        709
osc                269
wait_for_service    25
git_timed          730
dbsync              20
apt-get            625
=========================

This is your host IP address: 10.0.2.15
This is your host IPv6 address: ::1
Horizon is now available at http://10.0.2.15/dashboard
Keystone is serving at http://10.0.2.15/identity/
The default users are: admin and demo
The password: password
WARNING:
Using lib/neutron-legacy is deprecated, and it will be removed in the
future
With the removal of screen support, tail_log is deprecated and will be
removed after Queens
Services are running under systemd unit files.
For more information see:
https://docs.openstack.org/devstack/latest/systemd.html
DevStack Version: pike
Change: 0f75c57ad6b0011561777ae95b53612051149518 Merge "doc: How to remote-
pdb under systemd" 2017-09-08 02:24:21 +0000
OS Version: Ubuntu 16.04 xenial
2017-09-09 08:00:09.397 | stack.sh completed in 3033 seconds.
```

You can access Horizon to experience the web interface with OpenStack, or you can source openrc in your shell, and then use the OpenStack command-line tool to manage vms, networks, volumes, and images from there. Here's how you do it:

```
$ source openrc admin admin
```

Creating a KeyStone user

Now let's create a user and then assign it an admin role. These actions will be handled by KeyStone:

```
$ openstack domain list
+---------+---------+---------+--------------------+
| ID      | Name    | Enabled | Description        |
+---------+---------+---------+--------------------+
| default | Default | True    | The default domain |
+---------+---------+---------+--------------------+

$ openstack user create --domain default --password-prompt my-new-user
User Password:
Repeat User Password:
+---------------------+----------------------------------+
| Field               | Value                            |
+---------------------+----------------------------------+
| domain_id           | default                          |
| enabled             | True                             |
| id                  | 755bebd276f3451fa49f1194aee4dc20 |
| name                | my-new-user                      |
| options             | {}                               |
| password_expires_at | None                             |
+---------------------+----------------------------------+
```

Assign role to the user

We will assign an admin role to our user `my-new-user`:

```
$ openstack role add --domain default --user my-new-user admin

$ openstack user show my-new-user
+---------------------+----------------------------------+
| Field               | Value                            |
+---------------------+----------------------------------+
| domain_id           | default                          |
| enabled             | True                             |
| id                  | 755bebd276f3451fa49f1194aee4dc20 |
| name                | my-new-user                      |
| options             | {}                               |
| password_expires_at | None                             |
+---------------------+----------------------------------+
```

Creating a VM using Nova

Let's create a VM using Nova. We will use the cirros image from Glance, and the network from Neutron.

The available list of images in Glance are created by DevStack:

```
$ openstack image list
+------------------------------------+------------------------+--------+
| ID                                 | Name                   | Status |
+------------------------------------+------------------------+--------+
| f396a79e-7ccf-4354-8201-623e4a6ec115 | cirros-0.3.5-x86_64-disk | active |
| 0bc135f6-ebb5-4e8c-a44a-8b96954dfd93 | kubernetes/pause         | active |
+------------------------------------+------------------------+--------+
```

Also check the network list in Neutron created by the DevStack installation:

```
$ openstack network list
+--------------------------------------+---------+------------------------------------------------------------------+
| ID                                   | Name    | Subnets                                                          |
+--------------------------------------+---------+------------------------------------------------------------------+
| 765cab64-cfaf-49f7-8e51-194cb9f40b9e | public  | af1dc81e-30f6-48b1-8e4f-6c978fe863e8, f430926e-5648-4f88-a4bd-d009bf316dda |
| a021cfcd-cf4b-41f2-b30a-033c12c542e4 | private | 254b646c-e518-4418-bcef-08ea0a44f4bc, 93651473-3533-46a3-b77e-a2056d6f6ec5 |
+--------------------------------------+---------+------------------------------------------------------------------+
```

Nova provides a flavor that specifies the VM resources. Here is the list of flavors created by DevStack in Nova:

```
$ openstack flavor list
+-----+-----------+-------+------+-----------+-------+-----------+
| ID  | Name      |   RAM | Disk | Ephemeral | VCPUs | Is Public |
+-----+-----------+-------+------+-----------+-------+-----------+
| 1   | m1.tiny   |   512 |    1 |         0 |     1 | True      |
| 2   | m1.small  |  2048 |   20 |         0 |     1 | True      |
| 3   | m1.medium |  4096 |   40 |         0 |     2 | True      |
| 4   | m1.large  |  8192 |   80 |         0 |     4 | True      |
| 42  | m1.nano   |    64 |    0 |         0 |     1 | True      |
| 5   | m1.xlarge | 16384 |  160 |         0 |     8 | True      |
| 84  | m1.micro  |   128 |    0 |         0 |     1 | True      |
| c1  | cirros256 |   256 |    0 |         0 |     1 | True      |
| d1  | ds512M    |   512 |    5 |         0 |     1 | True      |
| d2  | ds1G      |  1024 |   10 |         0 |     1 | True      |
| d3  | ds2G      |  2048 |   10 |         0 |     2 | True      |
| d4  | ds4G      |  4096 |   20 |         0 |     4 | True      |
+-----+-----------+-------+------+-----------+-------+-----------+
```

We will create a keypair to be used to SSH to the VM created in Nova:

```
$ openstack keypair create --public-key ~/.ssh/id_rsa.pub mykey
+-------------+-------------------------------------------------+
| Field       | Value                                           |
+-------------+-------------------------------------------------+
| fingerprint | 98:0a:d5:70:30:34:16:06:79:3e:fc:33:14:b1:d9:b7 |
| name        | mykey                                           |
| user_id     | bbcd13444b1e4e4886eb8f36f4e80600                |
+-------------+-------------------------------------------------+
```

Let's create a VM using all the resources we listed previously:

```
$ openstack server create --flavor m1.tiny --image
f396a79e-7ccf-4354-8201-623e4a6ec115   --nic net-id=a021cfcd-cf4b-41f2-
b30a-033c12c542e4   --key-name mykey test-vm
+--------------------------------------+-------------------------------------
--------------------------------+
| Field                                | Value
|
+--------------------------------------+-------------------------------------
--------------------------------+
| OS-DCF:diskConfig                    | MANUAL
|
| OS-EXT-AZ:availability_zone          |
|
| OS-EXT-SRV-ATTR:host                 | None
```

```
|
| OS-EXT-SRV-ATTR:hypervisor_hostname | None
|
| OS-EXT-SRV-ATTR:instance_name       |
|
| OS-EXT-STS:power_state              | NOSTATE
|
| OS-EXT-STS:task_state               | scheduling
|
| OS-EXT-STS:vm_state                 | building
|
| OS-SRV-USG:launched_at              | None
|
| OS-SRV-USG:terminated_at            | None
|
| accessIPv4                          |
|
| accessIPv6                          |
|
| addresses                           |
|
| adminPass                           | dTTHcP3dByXR
|
| config_drive                        |
|
| created                             | 2017-09-09T08:36:55Z
|
| flavor                              | m1.tiny (1)
|
| hostId                              |
|
| id                                  | 6dc0c74c-7259-4730-929e-
b0f3d39a2c45                         |
| image                               | cirros-0.3.5-x86_64-disk
(f396a79e-7ccf-4354-8201-623e4a6ec115) |
| key_name                            | mykey
|
| name                                | test-vm
|
| progress                            | 0
|
| project_id                          | 7994b2ef08de4a05a5db61fcbee29506
|
| properties                          |
|
| security_groups                     | name='default'
|
| status                              | BUILD
```

```
|
| updated                           | 2017-09-09T08:36:55Z
|
| user_id                           | bbcd13444b1e4e4886eb8f36f4e80600
|
| volumes_attached                  |
|
+---------------------------------+---------------------------------------
---------------------------------+
```

Check the server list to verify whether the VM was launched successfully or not:

```
$ openstack server list
+---------------------------------+----------+--------+----------------
---------------------------------+--------------------------+--------
--+
| ID                              | Name     | Status | Networks
| Image                     | Flavor  |
+---------------------------------+--------+----------+--------------+
---------------------------------+--------------------------+--------
--+
| 6dc0c74c-7259-4730-929e-b0f3d39a2c45 | test-vm | ACTIVE |
private=10.0.0.8, fd26:4d99:7734:0:f816:3eff:feaf:e37b | cirros-0.3.5-
x86_64-disk | m1.tiny |
+---------------------------------+----------+--------+----------------
---------------------------------+--------------------------+--------
-+
```

Attach volume to VM

Now that our VM is running, let's try to do something more ambitious. We will now create a volume in Cinder and attach it to our running VM:

```
$ openstack availability zone list
+------------+--------------+
| Zone Name  | Zone Status  |
+------------+--------------+
| internal   | available    |
| nova       | available    |
| nova       | available    |
| nova       | available    |
| nova       | available    |
+------------+--------------+
$ openstack volume create --size 1 --availability-zone nova my-new-volume
+--------------------+-------------------------------------------+
| Field              | Value                                     |
```

```
+---------------------+-------------------------------------------+
| attachments         | []                                        |
| availability_zone   | nova                                      |
| bootable            | false                                     |
| consistencygroup_id | None                                      |
| created_at          | 2017-09-09T08:41:33.020340                |
| description         | None                                      |
| encrypted           | False                                     |
| id                  | 889c1f21-7ca5-4913-aa80-44182cea824e      |
| migration_status    | None                                      |
| multiattach         | False                                     |
| name                | my-new-volume                             |
| properties          |                                           |
| replication_status  | None                                      |
| size                | 1                                         |
| snapshot_id         | None                                      |
| source_volid        | None                                      |
| status              | creating                                  |
| type                | lvmdriver-1                               |
| updated_at          | None                                      |
| user_id             | bbcd13444b1e4e4886eb8f36f4e80600          |
+---------------------+-------------------------------------------+
```

Let's check the list of volumes in Cinder. We will see that our volume is created and is in an available state:

```
$ openstack volume list
+--------------------------------------+---------------+-----------+------+
+--------------+
| ID                                   | Name          | Status    | Size |
Attached to |
+--------------------------------------+---------------+-----------+------+
+--------------+
| 889c1f21-7ca5-4913-aa80-44182cea824e | my-new-volume | available |    1 |
|
+--------------------------------------+---------------+-----------+------+
+--------------+
```

Let's attach this volume to our VM:

```
$ openstack server add volume test-vm 889c1f21-7ca5-4913-aa80-44182cea824e
```

Verify whether the volume was attached:

```
$ openstack volume list
+------------------------------------------+-----------------+--------+------+---
----------------------------------+
| ID                                       | Name            | Status | Size |
Attached to                       |
+------------------------------------------+-----------------+--------+------+---
----------------------------------+
| 889c1f21-7ca5-4913-aa80-44182cea824e     | my-new-volume   | in-use |    1 |
Attached to test-vm on /dev/vdb   |
+------------------------------------------+-----------------+--------+------+---
----------------------------------+
```

You can see here that the volume is attached to our `test-vm` vm.

Uploading an image to Swift

We will try to upload an image to Swift. First, check the account details:

```
$ openstack object store account show
+------------+--------------------------------------+
| Field      | Value                                |
+------------+--------------------------------------+
| Account    | AUTH_8ef89519b0454b57a038b6f044fa0101 |
| Bytes      | 0                                    |
| Containers | 0                                    |
| Objects    | 0                                    |
+------------+--------------------------------------+
```

We will create an images container to store all our images. Similarly, we can create multiple containers inside an account with any logical name to store different types of data:

```
$ openstack container create images
+------------------------------------------+------------+----------------------
---------------+
| account                                  | container  | x-trans-id
|
+------------------------------------------+------------+----------------------
---------------+
| AUTH_8ef89519b0454b57a038b6f044fa0101    | images     |
tx3f28728ccbbe4fcabfe1b-0059b3af9b |
+------------------------------------------+------------+----------------------
---------------+
$ openstack container list
+---------+
```

```
| Name   |
+--------+
| images |
+--------+
```

Now that we have a container, let's upload an image to the container:

```
$ openstack object create images sunrise.jpeg
+--------------+-----------+----------------------------------+
| object       | container | etag                             |
+--------------+-----------+----------------------------------+
| sunrise.jpeg | images    | 243f98a9d31d140bb123e56624703106 |
+--------------+-----------+----------------------------------+
$ openstack object list images
+--------------+
| Name         |
+--------------+
| sunrise.jpeg |
+--------------+
$ openstack container show images
+--------------+---------------------------------------+
| Field        | Value                                 |
+--------------+---------------------------------------+
| account      | AUTH_8ef89519b0454b57a038b6f044fa0101 |
| bytes_used   | 2337288                               |
| container    | images                                |
| object_count | 1                                     |
+--------------+---------------------------------------+
```

You can see that the image was successfully uploaded to the Swift object store.

There are many more features that are available in OpenStack, which you can read about in the user guides available for each project.

Summary

In this chapter, we gave you a basic introduction to OpenStack and the components available in OpenStack. We discussed the components and the architecture of individual projects. Then we completed a DevStack installation to set up a development environment for running OpenStack. We then did some hands-on provisioning for a VM using Nova. This included adding a KeyStone user, assigning a role to them and attaching a volume to the VM after it was provisioned. Also, we looked at how we can use Swift to upload and download files. In the next chapter, we will look at the state of containerization in OpenStack.

4
Containerization in OpenStack

This chapter starts by explaining the need for containers in OpenStack. Then, it also explains the different processes going on inside OpenStack to support containers.

Containers are a pretty hot topic today. Users want to run their production workloads on containers along with virtual machines. They are popular for the following reasons:

- Containers provide immutable infrastructure models using the concept of packaging
- It's easy to develop and run microservices using containers
- They facilitate quicker development and testing of applications

The Linux kernel has supported containers for several years. Microsoft also recently started to support containers in the form of Windows Server containers and Hyper-V containers. As containers have evolved over time, so has OpenStack support for containers. OpenStack provides APIs to manage containers and their orchestration engines within the data centers.

In this chapter, we will discuss how OpenStack and containers fit together. This chapter covers the following topics:

- The need for containers in OpenStack
- Efforts within the OpenStack community to support containers

The need for containers in OpenStack

OpenStack is used by a large number of organizations. Cloud infrastructure vendors have called OpenStack an open source alternative to Amazon Web Services for organizations aiming to maintain a private cloud but with public cloud scalability and agility. OpenStack is popular for Linux-based **Infrastructure as a Service** (**IaaS**) offerings. As containers are gaining popularity, it's become necessary for OpenStack to provide various infrastructure resources such as computing, networking, and storage to containers. Rather than creating new vertical silos to manage containers in their data centers, developers and operators can find value in providing a cross plate-form API to manage virtual machines, containers, and bare metals.

Efforts within the OpenStack community to support containers

OpenStack provides the following:

- Compute resources
- Multi-tenant security and isolation
- Management and monitoring
- Storage and networking

The preceding mentioned services are needed for any cloud/data center management tool regardless of which containers, virtual machines, or bare metal servers are being used. Containers complement existing technology and bring a new set of benefits. OpenStack provides the support to run containers on bare metal or virtual machines.

In OpenStack, the following projects have taken initiative or provided support for containers and related technologies.

Nova

Nova is a compute service for OpenStack. Nova provides APIs to manage virtual machines. Nova supports the provisioning of machine containers using two libraries, that is, LXC and OpenVZ (Virtuozzo). These container related libraries are supported by libvirt, which Nova uses to manage virtual machines.

Heat

Heat is an orchestration service for OpenStack. Heat has supported the orchestration of Docker containers since the Icehouse release of OpenStack. Users need to enable plugins for Docker orchestration in Heat to use this feature.

Magnum

Magnum is a container infrastructure management service for OpenStack. Magnum provides APIs to deploy Kubernetes, Swarm, and Mesos clusters on OpenStack infrastructure. Magnum uses Heat templates to deploy these clusters on OpenStack. Users can use these clusters to run their containerized applications.

Zun

Zun is a container management service for OpenStack. Zun provides APIs to manage the life cycle of containers in OpenStack's cloud. Currently, Zun provides the support to run containers on bare metals, but in the future, it may provide the support to run containers on virtual machines created by Nova. Zun uses Kuryr to provide neutron networking to containers. Zun uses Cinder for providing persistent storage to containers.

Kuryr

Kuryr is a Docker network plugin that provides networking services to Docker containers using Neutron.

Kolla

Kolla is a project to which it deploys OpenStack Controller plane services within Docker containers. Kolla simplifies deployment and operations by packaging each controller service as a micro-service inside a Docker container.

Murano

Murano is an OpenStack project which provides an application catalog for app developers and cloud administrators to publish cloud-ready applications in a repository available within OpenStack Dashboard (**Horizon**) which can be run inside Docker or Kubernetes. It provides developers and operators with the ability to control the full life cycle of applications.

Fuxi

Fuxi is storage plugin for Docker containers that enables containers to use Cinder volume and Manila share as persistent storage inside them.

OpenStack-Helm

The **OpenStack-Helm** is another OpenStack project that provides a framework for operators and developers to deploy OpenStack on top of Kubernetes.

Summary

In this chapter, we learned why OpenStack should support containers. We also looked at the efforts which are going on in the OpenStack community to support containers.

In the next chapter, we will learn about Magnum (a container infrastructure management service in OpenStack) in detail. We will be also doing some hands-on exercises with COE management using Magnum in OpenStack.

5
Magnum – COE Management in OpenStack

This chapter will explain the OpenStack project for managing the **Container Orchestration Engine** (**COE**), Magnum. Magnum is the OpenStack project for managing infrastructure and for running containers on top of OpenStack, backed by different technologies. In this chapter, we will cover the following topics:

- Magnum introduction
- Concepts
- Key features
- Components
- Walk-through
- Magnum DevStack installation
- Managing COEs

Magnum introduction

Magnum is an OpenStack service that was created in 2014 by the OpenStack containers team to enable a **Container Orchestration Engine** (**COE**) offering the ability to deploy and manage containers as first-class resources in OpenStack.

Currently, Magnum supports Kubernetes, Apache Mesos, and Docker Swarm COEs. Magnum uses Heat to do the orchestration of these COEs on VMs or bare metals provisioned by OpenStack. It uses OS images that contain the required tools to run containers. Magnum offers KeyStone compatible APIs and a complete multi-tenant solution for managing your COEs on top of an OpenStack cluster.

A Magnum cluster is a set of various resources provided by different OpenStack services. It consists of a group of VMs provisioned by Nova, networks connecting these VMs created by Neutron, volumes attached to VMs created by Cinder, and so on. A Magnum cluster can also have some external resources depending on the options provided while creating a cluster. For example, we can create an external load balancer for our cluster by specifying the `-master-lb-enabled` option in the cluster template.

Some of the salient features of Magnum are:

- Provides a standard API for complete life cycle management of COEs
- Supports multiple COEs such as Kubernetes, Swarm, Mesos, and DC/OS
- Supports the ability to scale a cluster up or down
- Supports multi-tenancy for container clusters
- Different choices of container cluster deployment models: VM or bare-metal
- Provides KeyStone-based multi-tenant security and auth management
- Neutron based multi-tenant network control and isolation
- Supports Cinder to provide volume for containers
- Integrated with OpenStack
- Secure container cluster access (**Transport Layer Security (TLS)**) enabled
- Support for external infrastructure can also be used by the cluster, such as DNS, public network, public discovery service, Docker registry, load balancer, and so on
- Barbican provides the storage of secrets such as certificates used for TLS within the cluster
- Kuryr-based networking for container-level isolation

Concepts

Magnum has several different types of objects that form the Magnum system. In this section, we will learn about each of them in detail and also learn what they are used for in Magnum. Two important objects are the cluster and the cluster template. Here is a list of Magnum objects:

Cluster template

This was previously known as **Baymodel**. Cluster template is equivalent to a Nova flavor. An object stores template information about the cluster such as a keypair, image, and so on, and this is used to create new clusters consistently. Some parameters are relevant to the infrastructure of the cluster, while others are for the particular COE. Multiple cluster templates can exist for different COEs.

 A cluster template cannot be updated or deleted if is used by any cluster.

Cluster

This was previously known as **Bay**. It is a collection of node objects where work is scheduled. This node can be a VM or bare metal. Magnum deploys a cluster according to the attributes defined in the particular cluster template as well as a few additional parameters for the cluster. Magnum deploys the orchestration templates provided by the cluster driver to create and configure all of the necessary infrastructure where the COE runs. After a cluster is created, users can use the native CLIs of each COE to run their application on top of OpenStack.

Cluster driver

Cluster driver contains all of the necessary files that are needed for setting up a cluster. It contains a heat template defining the resources to be created for any cluster, scripts to install and configure services on the cluster, the version information of the driver, and the template definition.

Heat Stack Template

The **Heat Stack Template** (**HOT**) is a template that defines the resources which will form a COE cluster. Every COE type has a different template depending on the steps of its installation. This template is passed to Heat by Magnum to set up a full COE cluster.

Template definition

Template definition represents the mapping between Magnum attributes and Heat template attributes. It also has outputs that are consumed by Magnum. It indicates which cluster type it will use for a given cluster.

Certificate

Certificate is an object that represents the CA certificate for a cluster in Magnum. Magnum generates both server and client certificates while creating a cluster to provide a secure communication between Magnum services and COE services. The CA certificate and key are stored in Magnum for use by a user to access the cluster securely. Users need to generate a client certificate, a client key, and a Certificate Signing Request (CSR), and then send a request to Magnum to get it signed and also download the signing cert for accessing the cluster.

Service

Service is an object that stores the information about the `magnum-conductor` binary. This object contains information such as the host where the service is running, if the service is disabled or not, the last seen details, and so on. This information can be used by admins to see the status of the `magnum-conductor` services.

Stats

Magnum also manages the statistics of each project usage. This information is helpful for administration purposes. Stats objects contain some metrics about the current usage of any admin or user for a tenant or even for all active tenants. They provide information, such as the total number of clusters, nodes, and so on.

Quotas

Quotas is an object that stores the resource quota of any given project. Imposing quotas on resources puts a limitation on a number of resources that can be consumed, which helps to guarantee *fairness* or the fair distribution of resources at creation time. If a particular project needs more resources, the concept of quota provides the ability to increase the resource count on-demand, given that the system constraints are not exceeded. Quotas are tied closely to physical resources and are billable entities.

Key features

We have learned that Magnum provides various features in addition to the management of COE infrastructure in the previous section. In the following sections, we will talk about some of the advanced features present in Magnum.

External load balancer for Kubernetes

Magnum uses Flannel by default to provide networking for the resources in Kuberenetes. The pods and services can access each other and the external internet using this private container networking. However, these resources can't be accessed from an external network. To allow access from the external network, Magnum provides the support for setting up an external load balancer for a Kubernetes cluster.

Please refer to
`https://docs.openstack.org/magnum/latest/user/#steps-for-the-cluster-administrator` to set up a Kubernetes load balancer using Magnum.

Transport Layer Security

Magnum allows us to set up secure communication between a cluster's services and the outside world using TLS. The TLS communication in Magnum is employed at three layers:

- Communication between Magnum services and the cluster API endpoint.
- Communication between the cluster worker nodes and the master nodes.

- Communication between the end user and the cluster. End users use the native client libraries to interact with the cluster and with the certificates to communicate over a secure network. This applies to both a CLI and a program that uses a client for the particular cluster. Each client needs a valid certificate to authenticate and communicate with a cluster.

The first two cases are implemented internally by Magnum, and it creates, stores, and configures services to use the certificate for communication and are not exposed to the users. The last case involves the users creating a certificate, signing it, and then using it to access the cluster.

Magnum uses Barbican to store the certificates. This provides another level of security with the storage of a certificate. Magnum also supports other ways of storing certificates, such as storing them in a local filesystem of the conductor node or in the Magnum database.

Please refer to
`https://docs.openstack.org/magnum/latest/user/#interfacing-with-a-secure-cluster` for more details on how to configure clients to access the secure cluster.

Scaling

Scaling is yet another powerful feature of Magnum. Magnum supports the scaling of the cluster, whereas the scaling of containers is outside of Magnum's scope. Scaling a cluster can help users to either add or remove nodes from the cluster. While scaling up, Magnum creates a VM or bare metal, deploys the COE services on it, and then register it to the cluster. When scaling down, Magnum tries to remove the node with the least workload.

See the *Managing COEs* section to learn how to scale a cluster.

Storage

Magnum supports Cinder to provide block storage to the containers, which can either be persistent or ephemeral storage.

Ephemeral storage

All of the changes to a container's filesystem can be either stored in a local filesystem or in Cinder volume. This is the ephemeral storage which gets deleted after the container exits. Magnum provides additional Cinder volume to be used as ephemeral storage with containers. Users can specify the volume size in the cluster template using the `docker-volume-size` attribute. Also, users can select a different volume type, such as a device mapper, and overlay this with the `docker_volume_type` attribute.

Persistent storage

There can be a need to persist the container's data when it exits. A container can be mounted with Cinder volume for this purpose. When a container exits, the volume is unmounted, thus persisting the data.

There are a number of third-party volume drivers that support Cinder as the backend, such as Rexray and Flocker. Magnum currently supports Rexray as the volume driver for Swarm, and Mesos and Cinder for Kubernetes.

Notifications

Magnum generates notification about usage data. This data is useful for third-party applications for the purpose of billing, quota management, monitoring, and so on. To provide a standard format for the notification, Magnum uses the **Cloud Auditing Data Federation** (**CADF**) format.

Container monitoring

Magnum also supports the monitoring of containers. It collects metrics such as the container CPU load, the number of available Inodes, the cumulative count of bytes received, memory, CPU statistics of the node, and so on. The offered monitoring stack relies on the following set of containers and services present in the COE environment:

- cAdvisor
- Node exporter
- Prometheus
- Grafana

Users can set up this monitoring stack by specifying the given two configurable labels in the Magnum cluster template's definition that are `prometheus_monitoring` when set to True, the monitoring will be enabled and `grafana_admin_password` which the admin password.

Components

The diagram in the *Magnum Conductor* section shows the architecture of Magnum, which has two binaries named `magnum-api` and `magnum-conductor` that form the Magnum system. Magnum interacts with Heat to do the orchestration. This means Heat is the OpenStack component that talks to various other projects such as Nova, Neutron, and Cinder to set up the infrastructure for COE, and then it installs the COE on top of it. We will now learn about the detailed functions of the services.

Magnum API

Magnum API is a WSGI server that serves the API requests that the user sends to Magnum. The Magnum API has many controllers to handle a request for each of the resources:

- Baymodel
- Bay
- Certificate
- Cluster
- Cluster template
- Magnum services
- Quota
- Stats

Baymodel and Bay will be replaced by cluster and cluster templates respectively. Each of the controllers handle a request for specific resources. They validate the request for permissions, validate the OpenStack resources (such as validating if an image passed in the cluster template exists in Glance or not), create DB objects for the resource with the input data, and passes the request to `magnum-conductor` via the AMQP server. The call to `magnum-conductor` can be synchronous or asynchronous depending on the processing time taken by each of the operations.

For example, the list calls can be synchronous as they are not time-consuming, whereas the create requests can be asynchronous. Upon receiving a response from the conductor service, the `magnum-api` service returns the response to the user.

Magnum conductor

Magnum conductor is an RPC server that provides coordination and database query support for Magnum. It is stateless and horizontally scalable, meaning multiple instances of the conductor service can run at the same time. The `magnum-conductor` service selects the cluster driver and then sends the template files to the Heat service to do the installation, and finally updates the database with the object details.

Here is an architecture diagram for Magnum, which shows the different components in Magnum, what other OpenStack projects they communicate to, and the infrastructure provisioned for running any COE:

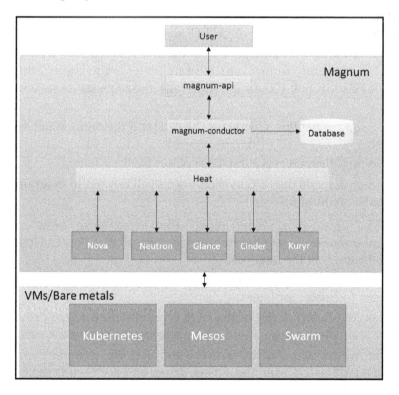

Walk-through

In this section, we will walk you through the process of a COE cluster being created by Magnum. This section deals with the request flow and the component interaction of various projects in OpenStack. Provisioning a cluster in Magnum involves interaction between multiple components inside OpenStack.

The request flow for provisioning a cluster in Magnum goes like this:

1. The user sends a REST API call to `magnum-api` for creating a cluster via a CLI or Horizon, with the authentication token received from KeyStone.
2. `magnum-api` receives the request and sends the request for the validation of token and access permission to KeyStone.
3. KeyStone validates the token and sends the updated authentications headers with roles and permissions.
4. `magnum-api` then validates the quota for the request. If the quota exceeds the hard limit, an exception is raised complaining that the *resource limit has exceeded* and the request exists with `403` HTTP status.
5. Then the validation of all OpenStack resources specified in the cluster template is done. For example, `magnum-api` talks to `nova-api` to check if the specified keypair exists or not. If the validation fails, the requests exists with `400` HTTP status.
6. `magnum-api` generates a name for the cluster if the name is not specified in the request.
7. `magnum-api` then creates a database object for the cluster.
8. `magnum-api` sends the RPC asynchronous call request to magnum-conductor to process the request further.
9. `magnum-conductor` picks the request from the message queue.
10. `magnum-conductor` sets the status of the cluster to `CREATE_IN_PROGRESS` and stores the entry in the database.
11. `magnum-conductor` creates the trustee, trust, and certificate for the cluster and sets them to cluster for later use.
12. Based on the cluster distribution, COE type, and server type provided in the cluster template, `magnum-conductor` selects a driver for the cluster.
13. `magnum-conductor` then extracts the template files, template, environment files, and heat parameters from the cluster driver and then sends the request to Heat to create the stack.

14. Heat then talks to multiple OpenStack services such as Nova, Neutron, and Cinder to set up the cluster and install the COE on top of it.

15. After the stack is created in Heat, the stack ID and cluster status is set to CREATE_COMPLETE in the Magnum database.

 There are periodic tasks in Magnum which sync the cluster status in the Magnum database at a specific time interval.

Magnum DevStack installation

To install Magnum with DevStack for development purposes, follow these steps:

1. Create a root directory for DevStack if needed:

```
$ sudo mkdir -p /opt/stack
$ sudo chown $USER /opt/stack
Clone DevStack repo:
$ git clone https://git.openstack.org/openstack-dev/devstack
/opt/stack/devstack
```

2. We will run DevStack with minimal local.conf settings required to enable Magnum, Heat, and Neutron:

```
$ cat > /opt/stack/devstack/local.conf << END
[[local|localrc]]
DATABASE_PASSWORD=password
RABBIT_PASSWORD=password
SERVICE_TOKEN=password
SERVICE_PASSWORD=password
ADMIN_PASSWORD=password
# magnum requires the following to be set correctly
PUBLIC_INTERFACE=eth1
# Enable barbican service and use it to store TLS certificates
enable_plugin barbican
https://git.openstack.org/openstack/barbican
enable_plugin heat
https://git.openstack.org/openstack/heat
# Enable magnum plugin after dependent plugins
enable_plugin magnum
https://git.openstack.org/openstack/magnum
# Optional:  uncomment to enable the Magnum UI plugin in
```

```
Horizon
#enable_plugin magnum-ui
https://github.com/openstack/magnum-ui
VOLUME_BACKING_FILE_SIZE=20G
END
```

 Please note that we have to use Barbican here for storing the TLS certificate generated by Magnum. For details, see the *Transport Layer Security* section under the *Key Features* section.

Also, make sure to use the appropriate interface for setup in `local.conf`.

3. Now, run DevStack:

```
$ cd /opt/stack/devstack
$ ./stack.sh
```

4. You will have a Magnum setup running. To verify the installation, check the list of Magnum services running:

```
$ magnum service-list
+----+----------+-------------------+-------+----------+-------------
-----+-----------------------
-+------------------------+
| id | host     | binary            | state | disabled |
disabled_reason | created_at
| updated_at              |
+----+----------+-------------------+-------+----------+-------------
-----+-----------------------
-+------------------------+
| 1  | devstack | magnum-conductor  | up    | False    | -
| 2017-09
19T11:14:12+00:00 | 2017-09-19T14:06:41+00:00 |
+----+----------+-------------------+-------+----------+-------------
-----+-----------------------
-+------------------------+
```

Managing COEs

Magnum provides seamless management for the life cycle of the cluster in OpenStack. The current operations are the basic CRUD operations, with some advance features such as the scaling of the cluster, setting up external load balancers, setting up a secure cluster with TLS, and so on. In this section, we will create a Swarm Cluster Template, use this template to create a Swarm cluster, and then, we will run some workloads on the cluster to verify our cluster status.

First, we will prepare our session to be able to use the various OpenStack clients including Magnum, Neutron, and Glance. Create a new shell and source the DevStack `openrc` script:

```
$ source /opt/stack/devstack/openrc admin admin
```

Create a keypair to use with the cluster template. This keypair will be used to ssh to the cluster nodes:

```
$ openstack keypair create --public-key ~/.ssh/id_rsa.pub testkey
+-------------+-------------------------------------------------+
| Field       | Value                                           |
+-------------+-------------------------------------------------+
| fingerprint | d2:8d:c8:d2:2a:82:fc:aa:98:17:5f:9b:22:08:8a:f7 |
| name        | testkey                                         |
| user_id     | 4360ea27027a4d9d97e749bba9698915                |
+-------------+-------------------------------------------------+
```

DevStack creates a Fedora Atomic micro-OS image in Glance for Magnum's use. Users can also create additional images in Glance for use in their cluster. Verify the image created in Glance:

```
$ openstack image list
+--------------------------------------+----------------------------------
-+--------+
| ID                                   | Name
| Status |
+--------------------------------------+----------------------------------
-+--------+
| 482bd0b4-883d-4fc5-bf26-a88a98ceddd1 | Fedora-Atomic-26-20170723.0.x86_64
| active |
| 6862d910-a320-499e-a19f-1dbcdc79455f | cirros-0.3.5-x86_64-disk
| active |
+--------------------------------------+----------------------------------
-+--------+
```

Now, create a Magnum cluster template with the swarm COE type. This is similar in nature to a Nova flavor and tells Magnum how to construct the cluster. The cluster template specifies all of the resources to be used in our cluster, such as a Fedora Atomic image, a Nova keypair, a network, and so on:

```
$ magnum cluster-template-create swarm-template --image Fedora-
Atomic-26-20170723.0.x86_64 --keypair testkey --external-network public --
flavor m1.small --docker-volume-size 5  --dns-nameserver 8.8.8.8 --coe
swarm
+-----------------------+------------------------------------------+
| Property              | Value                                    |
+-----------------------+------------------------------------------+
| insecure_registry     | -                                        |
| labels                | {}                                       |
| updated_at            | -                                        |
| floating_ip_enabled   | True                                     |
| fixed_subnet          | -                                        |
| master_flavor_id      | -                                        |
| uuid                  | 0963601a-50aa-4361-9f6f-5f64f0826da8     |
| no_proxy              | -                                        |
| https_proxy           | -                                        |
| tls_disabled          | False                                    |
| keypair_id            | testkey                                  |
| public                | False                                    |
| http_proxy            | -                                        |
| docker_volume_size    | 5                                        |
| server_type           | vm                                       |
| external_network_id   | public                                   |
| cluster_distro        | fedora-atomic                            |
| image_id              | Fedora-Atomic-26-20170723.0.x86_64       |
| volume_driver         | -                                        |
| registry_enabled      | False                                    |
| docker_storage_driver | devicemapper                             |
| apiserver_port        | -                                        |
| name                  | swarm-template                           |
| created_at            | 2017-09-19T13:06:28+00:00                |
| network_driver        | docker                                   |
| fixed_network         | -                                        |
| coe                   | swarm                                    |
| flavor_id             | m1.small                                 |
| master_lb_enabled     | False                                    |
| dns_nameserver        | 8.8.8.8                                  |
+-----------------------+------------------------------------------+
```

Verify the cluster template creation by using the following command:

```
$ magnum cluster-template-list
+----------------------------------------+-----------------+
| uuid                                   | name            |
+----------------------------------------+-----------------+
| 0963601a-50aa-4361-9f6f-5f64f0826da8   | swarm-template  |
+----------------------------------------+-----------------+
```

Create a cluster using the preceding template. This cluster will result in a group of VMs to be created with Docker Swarm installed on them:

```
$ magnum cluster-create swarm --cluster-template swarm-template --node-
count 1
Request to create cluster f42f5dfc-a2d0-4f89-9af1-566c666727c3 has been
accepted.
```

Clusters will have an initial status of CREATE_IN_PROGRESS. Magnum will update the status to CREATE_COMPLETE when it is done creating the cluster.

Heat can be used to see detailed information on the status of a stack or specific cluster.

To check the list of all cluster stacks, use the following:

```
$ openstack stack list
+----------------------------------------+--------------------+--------------
--------------------+--------------------+----------------------+-----------
---+
| ID                                     | Stack Name         | Project
| Stack Status       | Creation Time      | Updated Time |
+----------------------------------------+--------------------+--------------
--------------------+--------------------+----------------------+-----------
----+
| 9d39e877-32ff-4904-a349-727274caee68   | swarm-5g5ilw3lak6p |
8c4a19b957904085992dd800621459b6 | CREATE_IN_PROGRESS |
2017-09-19T13:07:52Z | None          |
+----------------------------------------+--------------------+--------------
--------------------+--------------------+----------------------+-----------
----+
```

To see the details of cluster, do the following:

```
$ magnum cluster-show swarm
+-----------------------------+-----------------------------------------------
-----------------------------------------------------------------------------
-----------------------------------------------------------------------------
-----------------------------------------------------------------------------
-----------------------------------------------------------------------------
-------------------------------------------------+
| Property                    | Value
|
+-----------------------------+-----------------------------------------------
-----------------------------------------------------------------------------
-----------------------------------------------------------------------------
-----------------------------------------------------------------------------
-------------------------------------------------+
| labels                      | {}
|
| updated_at                  | 2017-09-19T13:16:41+00:00
|
| keypair                     | testkey
|
| node_count                  | 1
|
| uuid                        | f42f5dfc-a2d0-4f89-9af1-566c666727c3
|
| api_address                 | https://172.24.4.4:6443
|
| master_addresses            | ['172.24.4.2']
|
| create_timeout              | 60
|
| status                      | CREATE_COMPLETE
|
| docker_volume_size          | 5
|
| master_count                | 1
|
| node_addresses              | ['172.24.4.3']
|
| status_reason               | Stack CREATE completed successfully
|
| coe_version                 | 1.2.5
|
| cluster_template_id         | 0963601a-50aa-4361-9f6f-5f64f0826da8
|
| name                        | swarm
```

```
|
| stack_id              | 9d39e877-32ff-4904-a349-727274caee68
|
| created_at            | 2017-09-19T13:07:46+00:00
|
| discovery_url         |
https://discovery.etcd.io/af18b93f0d1b64db0d803a1c76e4d0d0
|
| container_version     | 1.12.6
|
+---------------------+------------------------------------------------
-----------------------------------------------------------------------
-----------------------------------------------------------------------
-----------------------------------------------------------------------
-----------------------------------------------------------------------
-------------------------------------------+
```

We now need to set up the Docker CLI to use the swarm cluster we have created with the appropriate credentials.

Create a `dir` to store `certs` and `cd`. The `DOCKER_CERT_PATH` env variable is consumed by Docker, which expects `ca.pem`, `key.pem`, and `cert.pem` to be in that directory:

```
$ export DOCKER_CERT_PATH=~/.docker
$ mkdir -p ${DOCKER_CERT_PATH}
$ cd ${DOCKER_CERT_PATH}
```

Generate an RSA key:

```
$ openssl genrsa -out key.pem 4096
```

Create `openssl` config to help generated a CSR:

```
$ cat > client.conf << END
[req]
distinguished_name = req_distinguished_name
req_extensions     = req_ext
prompt = no
[req_distinguished_name]
CN = Your Name
[req_ext]
extendedKeyUsage = clientAuth
END
```

Run the `openssl req` command to generate the CSR:

```
$ openssl req -new -days 365 -config client.conf -key key.pem -out
client.csr
```

Now that you have your client CSR, use the Magnum CLI to get it signed and also download the signing cert:

```
$ magnum ca-sign --cluster swarm-cluster --csr client.csr > cert.pem
$ magnum ca-show --cluster swarm-cluster > ca.pem
```

Set the CLI to use TLS. This `env var` is consumed by Docker:

```
$ export DOCKER_TLS_VERIFY="1"
```

Set the correct host to use, which is the public IP address of the Swarm API server endpoint.

This `env var` is consumed by Docker:

```
$ export DOCKER_HOST=$(magnum cluster-show swarm-cluster | awk '/
api_address /{print substr($4,7)}')
```

Next, we will create a container in this Swarm cluster. This container will ping the address `8.8.8.8` four times:

```
$ docker run --rm -it cirros:latest ping -c 4 8.8.8.8
```

You should see a similar output to the following:

```
PING 8.8.8.8 (8.8.8.8): 56 data bytes
64 bytes from 8.8.8.8: seq=0 ttl=40 time=25.513 ms
64 bytes from 8.8.8.8: seq=1 ttl=40 time=25.348 ms
64 bytes from 8.8.8.8: seq=2 ttl=40 time=25.226 ms
64 bytes from 8.8.8.8: seq=3 ttl=40 time=25.275 ms
--- 8.8.8.8 ping statistics ---
4 packets transmitted, 4 packets received, 0% packet loss
round-trip min/avg/max = 25.226/25.340/25.513 ms
```

After a cluster is created, you can dynamically add or remove node(s) to or from the cluster by updating the `node_count` attribute. For example, to add one more node, do the following:

```
$ magnum cluster-update swarm replace node_count=2
```

Clusters will have a status of UPDATE_IN_PROGRESS while the process of the update continues. After the completion of update, the status will be updated to UPDATE_COMPLETE. Reducing `node_count` removes all of the existing pods/containers on the nodes that were deleted. Magnum tries to delete the node with the least workload.

Summary

In this chapter, we learned about the OpenStack container infrastructure management service, Magnum, in detail. We looked into the different objects in Magnum. Then, we learned about the components and architecture of Magnum. Then, we provided a detailed overview of the user request workflow in Magnum.

Finally, we looked at how to install a development setup for Magnum using DevStack and then did a hands-on exercise using Magnum CLI to create a Docker Swarm COE.

In the next chapter, we will learn about Zun, which is a container management service for OpenStack.

6
Zun – Container Management in OpenStack

In this chapter, we will learn about the OpenStack project for managing containers, Zun. Zun is the only solution available in OpenStack that allows its users to manage their application containers, backed by different technologies with the goodness of other OpenStack components such as Cinder, Glance, and Neutron. Zun provides a strong platform for running containerized applications on top of OpenStack IaaS.

This chapter will cover the following topics:

- Introduction to Zun
- Concepts
- Key features
- Components
- Walk-through
- Zun DevStack installation
- Managing containers

Introduction to Zun

Zun is an OpenStack service started in the Mitaka cycle developed by the members of the Magnum team. A decision was made at the OpenStack Austin Summit in 2016 to create a new project to allow for the management of containers and let the Magnum Container Infrastructure Management service manage only the infrastructure for running containers. The result was the Zun project.

Zun is a container management service for OpenStack that provides APIs to manage containers abstracted by different technologies at the backend. Zun supports Docker as the container runtime tool. Today, Zun integrates with many OpenStack services such as Neutron for networking, Glance for managing container images, and Cinder for providing volume to the containers.

Zun has various add-ons over Docker, which makes it a powerful solution for container management. Here is a list of some of the salient features of Zun:

- Provides a standard API for the complete life cycle management of containers
- Provides KeyStone-based multi-tenant security and auth management
- Supports Docker with runc and clear container for managing containers
- The support of clear container provides higher security by packing an individual container in a VM with a small footprint
- Supports Cinder to provide volume for containers
- Kuryr-based networking for container-level isolation
- Supports container orchestration via Heat
- Container composition known as capsules lets user run multiple containers with related resources as a single unit
- Supports the SR-IOV feature that enables the sharing of a physical PCIe device to be shared across VMs and containers
- Supports interactive sessions with containers
- Zun allows users to run heavy workloads with dedicated resources by exposing CPU sets

Concepts

In the following sections, we will look at the various objects available in the Zun system.

Containers

The container is the most important resource in Zun. A container in Zun represents any application container run by the users. A container object stores information such as the image, command, workdir, host, and so on. Zun is an extendable solution; it can support other container runtime tools as well. It has a driver-based implementation for each tool. The Docker driver in Zun manages containers via Docker. Containers in Zun support many advanced operations including CRUD operations such as create, start, stop, pause, delete, update, kill, and so on.

Images

Images in Zun are container images. These images are managed either by Docker Hub or Glance. Users can download the image and save them to Glance prior to container creation to save time. An image object stores information such as the image name, tag, size, and so on. Operations supported for images are upload, download, update, and search images.

Services

A service in Zun represents the `zun-compute` service. Zun can have multiple instances of `zun-compute` services running to support scalability. This object is used to establish the state of the compute services running in the Zun cluster. A service stores information such as the state, enabled or disabled, last known time, and so on.

Hosts

A host in Zun represents the compute node's resources. The compute node is the physical machine where the containers run. This is used to establish the list of available, used resources in Zun. A host object in Zun stores useful information about a compute node such as total memory, free memory, total number of running, stopped, or paused containers, total CPUs, free CPUs, and so on.

Capsules

A capsule in Zun represents a composition unit which contains multiple containers and other related resources. Containers in a capsule share resources among themselves and are tightly coupled to work together as a single unit. A capsule object stores information such as the container list, CPU, memory, and so on.

Container drivers

Zun is designed to be an extendable solution for managing containers on top of OpenStack. Zun supports Docker to manage containers. It aims to support multiple other tools in the future as well, such as Rocket. To support this, Zun has a collection of container drivers, which can be implemented with many other runtime tools and made available as solutions with Zun. Users can choose to manage their containers with their choice of tool.

Image drivers

We have learned that Zun can support multiple container runtime tools to manage containers. Similarly, it supports multiple image drivers for the managing of container images such as Glance driver and Docker driver. The image driver is also configurable; users can choose any of the available solutions for their use case.

Network drivers

The ability to communicate between two containers and between a container and VM is provided by the network driver in Zun. Zun has a Kuryr driver for managing all of the network resources for containers. It supports operations such as creating and deleting a network, connecting to and disconnecting a container from a network, and so on.

Key features

Zun has many advanced features in addition to the basic management of containers. In this section, we will talk about some of the advanced features present in Zun. There are many other features in progress, such as SRIOV networking, PCIe devices, and so on, which are referred to in the Zun documentation.

Cinder integration

Zun supports the attaching of persistent storage to the containers which exist even after the container exits. This storage can be used to store large amounts of data outside the host, which is more reliable if the host goes down. This support is enabled in Zun via Cinder. Users can mount and unmount Cinder volumes to their containers. The users first need to create the volume in Cinder and then provide the volume while creating the container.

Container composition

Zun supports the creation of multiple containers as a single unit. This unit is known as a capsule in Zun. This concept is very similar to pods in Kubernetes. A capsule contains multiple containers and all of the related resources such as network and storage, tightly coupled. All of the containers in a capsule are scheduled on the same host and share resources such as the Linux namespaces, CGroups, and so on.

Kuryr networking

A container created by Zun can interact with the VMs created by Nova. This feature is provided by `Kuryr-libnetwork`. It interacts with Neutron to create the necessary network resources for the container and provides a communication path for other OpenStack resources.

Container sandbox

Zun has a collection of sandbox containers. A sandbox is a container that has all of the IaaS resources associated with it, such as ports, IP addresses, volumes, and so on. The aim of the sandbox is to decouple the overhead of managing these IaaS resources from the application containers. A sandbox can manage single or multiple containers and provide all of the needed resources.

CPU sets

Zun allows its users to run a high-performance container with dedicated resources. Zun exposes its host capabilities to the users, and users can specify the required CPU while creating a container.

The scheduler filters a node with the available resource and provisions the container on that node. The host information is updated in the database to reflect the updated resources.

Components

The diagram in the *Zun WebSocket proxy* section shows the architecture of Zun. Zun has two binaries: `zun-api` and `zun-compute`. These two services together carry the whole life cycle of container management of containers. These services interact with other OpenStack services such as Glance for the container images, Cinder for providing volume to the containers, and Neutron for the connectivity between containers and the outside world. The request for containers is finally communicated to the Docker services running on the compute node. Docker then creates the container for the users.

zun-api

`zun-api` is a WSGI server that serves the users' API requests. For every resource in Zun, there are separate handlers:

- Container
- Host
- Images
- Zun services

Each of the controllers handle a request for specific resources. They validate the request for permissions, validate the OpenStack resources including validating if the image is present in Docker Hub or Glance, and create a DB object for the resource with the input data. The request is forwarded to the compute manager. Upon receiving a response from the `zun-compute` service, the `zun-api` service returns the response to the user.

Zun scheduler

The scheduler in Zun is not an RPC service. It is a simple Python class which applies a filter on the compute nodes and picks up the appropriate node for serving the request. The compute manager then passes the request to the selected `zun-compute` via an RPC call. The call to `zun-compute` can be synchronous or asynchronous depending on the processing time taken by each of the operations. For example, the list calls can be synchronous as they are not time-consuming, whereas the create requests can be asynchronous.

zun-compute

The `zun-compute` service is the main component of the Zun system. It performs most of the backend operations, hiding all the complexities. `zun-compute` selects an appropriate driver for serving each request and creates the related resources for containers, such as network resources. It then passes the request to the driver with all the required information. `zun-compute` talks to multiple projects for various resources such as Glance for the container images and Neutron for the network resources.

Zun WebSocket proxy

Zun has a WebSocket proxy service for running containers in interactive mode. This service establishes a secure connection with the container to run any commands inside it:

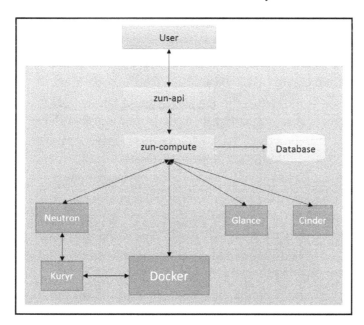

Walk-through

In this section, we will walk you through how a container is created in Zun and how the request flows from the user to the Docker which creates the container. Zun interacts with multiple other OpenStack services for resources needed for the container.

The request flow for creating a container in Zun is as follows:

1. The user sends a REST API call to the `zun-api` service for creating a cluster via a CLI or Horizon, with the authentication token received from KeyStone.
2. `zun-api` receives the request and sends the request for the validation of token and access permission to KeyStone.
3. KeyStone validates the token and sends updated authentications headers with roles and permissions.
4. `zun-api` then parses some parameters from the request, such as the security group, memory, and runtime, and validates them.
5. The requested network is created by `zun-api`. `zun-api` sends a request to Neutron to ensure the requested network or port is usable. If not, `zun-api` sends another request to Neutron to search the available network and creates a new Docker network for the container.
6. `zun-api` then checks whether the requested image is available or not. If the image is not found, the request fails with 400 HTTP status.
7. `zun-api` generates a name for the container if not provided in the request.
8. `zun-api` then creates a database object for the container.
9. `zun-api` sends the request to the compute API manager. The compute manager looks for the destination compute node from the scheduler.
10. `zun-api` then sends the RPC asynchronous call request to `zun-compute`, selected in the previous step, to process the request further.
11. `zun-compute` picks the request from the message queue.
12. `zun-compute` sets the `task_state` of the container to `IMAGE_PULLING` and stores the entry in the database.
13. `zun-compute` calls the image driver to download the image.
14. After the image is downloaded successfully, the `task_state` is now set to `CONTAINER_CREATING` in the database.
15. Now, `zun-compute` claims the resources required for the container and updates the compute node resource table with the required information.
16. Finally, the request to the Docker is sent to create the container with all of the required parameters.
17. The Docker driver creates the container, sets the status to `CREATED` and `status_reason` to `None`, and saves the container object in the database.
18. The `task_state` is set to `None` upon successful completion of the container.

There are periodic tasks in Zun which sync the container status in the Zun database at a specific time interval.

Zun DevStack installation

We will now look at how to install a development setup of Zun using DevStack:

Create a root directory for DevStack if needed:

```
$ sudo mkdir -p /opt/stack
$ sudo chown $USER /opt/stack
```

To clone DevStack repository, do the following:

```
$ git clone https://git.openstack.org/openstack-dev/devstack
/opt/stack/devstack
```

Now, create a minimal `local.conf` for running the DevStack setup. We will enable the following plugins to create a Zun setup:

- `devstack-plugin-container`: This plugin installs Docker
- `kuryr-libnetwork`: This is the Docker libnetwork driver that uses Neutron to provide networking services

```
$ cat > /opt/stack/devstack/local.conf << END
[[local|localrc]]
HOST_IP=$(ip addr | grep 'state UP' -A2 | tail -n1 | awk '{print $2}' |
cut -f1  -d'/')
DATABASE_PASSWORD=password
RABBIT_PASSWORD=password
SERVICE_TOKEN=password
SERVICE_PASSWORD=password
ADMIN_PASSWORD=password
enable_plugin devstack-plugin-container
https://git.openstack.org/openstack/devstack-plugin-container
enable_plugin zun https://git.openstack.org/openstack/zun
enable_plugin kuryr-libnetwork
https://git.openstack.org/openstack/kuryr-libnetwork
# Optional:  uncomment to enable the Zun UI plugin in Horizon
# enable_plugin zun-ui https://git.openstack.org/openstack/zun-ui
END
```

Now, run DevStack:

```
$ cd /opt/stack/devstack
$ ./stack.sh
```

Create a new shell and source the DevStack openrc script to use Zun CLI:

```
$ source /opt/stack/devstack/openrc admin admin
```

Now, let's verify the Zun installation by looking at the service list:

```
$ zun service-list
+----+--------+-------------+-------+----------+-----------------+---------
------------------+--------------------------+
| Id | Host   | Binary      | State | Disabled | Disabled Reason | Created
At                | Updated At               |
+----+--------+-------------+-------+----------+-----------------+---------
------------------+--------------------------+
| 1  | galvin | zun-compute | up    | False    | None            |
2017-10-10 11:22:50+00:00 | 2017-10-10 11:37:03+00:00 |
+----+--------+-------------+-------+----------+-----------------+---------
------------------+--------------------------+
```

Let's look at the host-list, which also shows the compute nodes being registered for use in Zun:

```
$ zun host-list
+--------------------------------------+----------+-----------+------+-----
----------------+--------+
| uuid                                 | hostname | mem_total | cpus | os
| labels |
+--------------------------------------+----------+-----------+------+-----
----------------+--------+
| 08fb3f81-d88e-46a1-93b9-4a2c18ed1f83 | galvin   | 3949      | 1    |
Ubuntu 16.04.3 LTS | {}     |
+--------------------------------------+----------+-----------+------+-----
----------------+--------+
```

We can see that we have one compute node, which is the host machine itself. Now, let's also look at the available resources in the host:

```
$ zun host-show galvin
+-------------------+-------------------------------------------------------
------------------------------------------------------------------------
-----------------------------------------------------------------+
| Property          | Value
|
+-------------------+-------------------------------------------------------
```

```
----------------------------------------------------------------------
--------------------------------------------------------------------+
| hostname         | galvin
|
| uuid             | 08fb3f81-d88e-46a1-93b9-4a2c18ed1f83
|
| links            | ["{u'href':
u'http://10.0.2.15/v1/hosts/08fb3f81-d88e-46a1-93b9-4a2c18ed1f83', u'rel':
u'self'}", "{u'href':
u'http://10.0.2.15/hosts/08fb3f81-d88e-46a1-93b9-4a2c18ed1f83', u'rel':
u'bookmark'}"] |
| kernel_version   | 4.10.0-28-generic
|
| labels           | {}
|
| cpus             | 1
|
| mem_total        | 3949
|
| total_containers | 0
|
| os_type          | linux
|
| os               | Ubuntu 16.04.3 LTS
|
| architecture     | x86_64
|
+------------ ------+------------------------------------------------
----------------------------------------------------------------------
------------------------------------------------------------------+
```

We can see that the `zun-compute` service is running. The current setup only installs one compute service; you can install a multi-node Zun setup also. Please refer to `https://github.com/openstack/zun/blob/master/doc/source/contributor/quickstart.rst` for more details.

Managing containers

Now that we have a Zun setup running, we will try to do some operations on containers in this section.

We will now create a container in Zun. But before that, let's check the Docker status:

```
$ sudo docker ps -a
CONTAINER ID          IMAGE
COMMAND                      CREATED                    STATUS
PORTS                 NAMES
```

We can see that no container exists now. Now, let's create the container:

```
$ zun create --name test cirros ping -c 4 8.8.8.8
+-------------------+-------------------------------------------------------
-------------------------------------------------------------------------
-------------------------------------------------------------------------
---+
| Property          | Value
|
+-------------------+-------------------------------------------------------
-------------------------------------------------------------------------
-------------------------------------------------------------------------
---+
| addresses         |
|
| links             | ["{u'href':
u'http://10.0.2.15/v1/containers/f78e778a-ecbd-42d3-bc77-ac50334c8e57',
u'rel': u'self'}", "{u'href':
u'http://10.0.2.15/containers/f78e778a-ecbd-42d3-bc77-ac50334c8e57',
u'rel': u'bookmark'}"] |
| image             | cirros
|
| labels            | {}
|
| networks          |
|
| security_groups   | None
|
| image_pull_policy | None
|
| uuid              | f78e778a-ecbd-42d3-bc77-ac50334c8e57
|
| hostname          | None
|
| environment       | {}
|
| memory            | None
|
| status            | Creating
|
| workdir           | None
```

```
|
| auto_remove        | False
|
| status_detail      | None
|
| host               | None
|
| image_driver       | None
|
| task_state         | None
|
| status_reason      | None
|
| name               | test
|
| restart_policy     | None
|
| ports              | None
|
| command            | "ping" "-c" "4" "8.8.8.8"
|
| runtime            | None
|
| cpu                | None
|
| interactive        | False
|
+-------------------+------------------------------------------------------
-----------------------------------------------------------------------------
-----------------------------------------------------------------------------
---+
```

Now, let's look at the Zun list to check the container status:

```
stack@galvin:~/devstack$ zun list
+--------------------------------------+------+--------+----------+--------
-------+-----------+-------+
| uuid                                 | name | image  | status   |
task_state    | addresses | ports |
+--------------------------------------+------+--------+----------+--------
-------+-----------+-------+
| f78e778a-ecbd-42d3-bc77-ac50334c8e57 | test | cirros | Creating |
image_pulling |           | []    |
+--------------------------------------+------+--------+----------+--------
-------+-----------+-------+
```

We can see that the container is in a creating state. Let's check the container in Docker as well:

```
$ sudo docker ps -a
CONTAINER ID         IMAGE
COMMAND                  CREATED           STATUS
PORTS                NAMES
cbd2c94d6273         cirros:latest
"ping -c 4 8.8.8.8"      38 seconds ago    Created
zun-f78e778a-ecbd-42d3-bc77-ac50334c8e57
```

Now, let's start the container and look at the logs:

```
$ zun start test
Request to start container test has been accepted.
$ zun logs test
PING 8.8.8.8 (8.8.8.8): 56 data bytes
64 bytes from 8.8.8.8: seq=0 ttl=40 time=25.513 ms
64 bytes from 8.8.8.8: seq=1 ttl=40 time=25.348 ms
64 bytes from 8.8.8.8: seq=2 ttl=40 time=25.226 ms
64 bytes from 8.8.8.8: seq=3 ttl=40 time=25.275 ms
--- 8.8.8.8 ping statistics ---
4 packets transmitted, 4 packets received, 0% packet loss
round-trip min/avg/max = 25.226/25.340/25.513 ms
```

Let's do some advanced operations with the container. We will now create an interactive container with Zun:

```
$ zun run -i --name new ubuntu /bin/bash
+-------------------+-------------------------------------------------------
------------------------------------------------------------------------
------------------------------------------------------------------------
---+
| Property          | Value
|
+-------------------+-------------------------------------------------------
------------------------------------------------------------------------
------------------------------------------------------------------------
---+
| addresses         |
|
| links             | ["{u'href':
u'http://10.0.2.15/v1/containers/dd6764ee-7e86-4cf8-bae8-b27d6d1b3225',
u'rel': u'self'}", "{u'href':
u'http://10.0.2.15/containers/dd6764ee-7e86-4cf8-bae8-b27d6d1b3225',
u'rel': u'bookmark'}"] |
| image             | ubuntu
|
```

```
| labels            | {}
|
| networks          |
|
| security_groups   | None
|
| image_pull_policy | None
|
| uuid              | dd6764ee-7e86-4cf8-bae8-b27d6d1b3225
|
| hostname          | None
|
| environment       | {}
|
| memory            | None
|
| status            | Creating
|
| workdir           | None
|
| auto_remove       | False
|
| status_detail     | None
|
| host              | None
|
| image_driver      | None
|
| task_state        | None
|
| status_reason     | None
|
| name              | new
|
| restart_policy    | None
|
| ports             | None
|
| command           | "/bin/bash"
|
| runtime           | None
|
| cpu               | None
|
| interactive       | True
|
+-------------------+-------------------------------------------------
----------------------------------------------------------------------
```

```
------------------------------------------------------------------------
---+
Waiting for container start
Waiting for container start
Waiting for container start
Waiting for container start
Waiting for container start
Waiting for container start
Waiting for container start
Waiting for container start
Waiting for container start
Waiting for container start
connected to dd6764ee-7e86-4cf8-bae8-b27d6d1b3225, press Enter to continue
type ~. to disconnect
root@81142e581b10:/#
root@81142e581b10:/# ls
bin  boot  dev  etc  home  lib  lib64  media  mnt  opt  proc  root  run
sbin  srv  sys  tmp  usr  var
root@81142e581b10:/# exit
exit
```

Now, let's delete the container:

```
$ zun delete test
Request to delete container test has been accepted.

$ zun list
+---------------------------------------+-------+---------+---------+---------
---+----------------------------+-------+
| uuid                                  | name  | image   | status  |
task_state | addresses                  | ports |
+---------------------------------------+-------+---------+---------+---------
---+----------------------------+-------+
| dd6764ee-7e86-4cf8-bae8-b27d6d1b3225  | new   | ubuntu  | Stopped | None
| 172.24.4.11, 2001:db8::d | []      |
+---------------------------------------+-------+---------+---------+---------
---+----------------------------+-------+
```

We will now look at some commands to see how images are managed in Zun. Download an Ubuntu image:

```
$ zun pull ubuntu
+----------+------------------------------------------------------------
----------------------------------------------------------------------
--------------------------------------------------------------+
| Property | Value
|
+----------+------------------------------------------------------------
----------------------------------------------------------------------
--------------------------------------------------------------+
| uuid     | 9b34875a-50e1-400c-a74b-028b253b35a4
|
| links    | ["{u'href':
u'http://10.0.2.15/v1/images/9b34875a-50e1-400c-a74b-028b253b35a4', u'rel':
u'self'}", "{u'href':
u'http://10.0.2.15/images/9b34875a-50e1-400c-a74b-028b253b35a4', u'rel':
u'bookmark'}"] |
| repo     | ubuntu
|
| image_id | None
|
| tag      | latest
|
| size     | None
|
+----------+------------------------------------------------------------
----------------------------------------------------------------------
--------------------------------------------------------------+
```

Let's look at the list of images in Zun now:

```
stack@galvin:~/devstack$ zun image-list
+--------------------------------------+----------+--------+--------+------
+
| uuid                                 | image_id | repo   | tag    | size
|
+--------------------------------------+----------+--------+--------+------
+
| 9b34875a-50e1-400c-a74b-028b253b35a4 | None     | ubuntu | latest | None
|
+--------------------------------------+----------+--------+--------+------
+
```

Summary

In this chapter, we learned about the OpenStack container management service, Zun. We looked into the different objects in Zun. Then, we also learned about the components and the architecture of Zun. The chapter also provided a detailed overview of the workflow of a user request to manage containers in Zun. Then, we looked at how to install a development setup in Zun using DevStack, and we did a hands-on exercise using Zun CLI to create a container and start and stop various other operations on containers. In the next chapter, we will learn about Kuryr, which provides the networking resources to containers using Neutron.

7
Kuryr – Container Plugin for OpenStack Networking

In this chapter, we will be learning about Kuryr, an OpenStack project for container networking. This chapter will cover the following topics:

- Introducing Kuryr
- Kuryr architecture
- Installation of Kuryr
- Walk-through

Introducing Kuryr

Kuryr is named after the Czech word which means a courier. It is a Docker network plugin that uses OpenStack Neutron to provide networking services to Docker containers. It maps container network abstractions to OpenStack neutron APIs. This provides the ability to connect VMs, containers, and bare metal servers to the same virtual network in a seamless management experience, and provides consistent networking for all three. Kuryr can be deployed using a Python package or a container using Kolla. It provides the following features to containers using a neutron as a provider:

- Security groups
- Subnet pools
- NAT (SNAT/DNAT, Floating IP)
- Port security (ARP spoofing)
- Quality of Service (QoS)

- Quota management
- Neutron pluggable IPAM
- Well-integrated COE load balancing via a neutron
- FWaaS for containers

Kuryr architecture

In the following sections, we will look at the Kuryr architecture.

Mapping the Docker libnetwork to the neutron API

The following diagram shows the Kuryr architecture that maps the Docker libnetwork networking model to the neutron API. Kuryr maps **libnetwork** APIs and creates the appropriate resource in the neutron, which explains why the **Neutron API** can also be used for container networking:

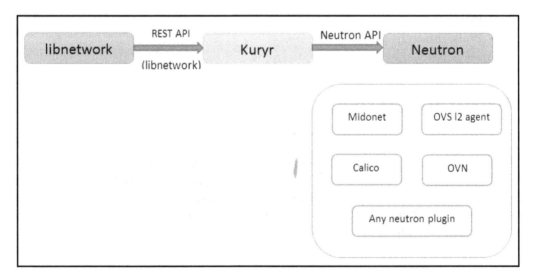

Providing the generic VIF-Binding infrastructure

Kuryr provides a generic VIF binding mechanism for the various port types which will be received from the Docker namespace and will be attached to the networking solution infrastructure depending on its type, for example, **Linux bridge port**, **Open vSwitch port**, **Midonet port**, and so on. The following diagram represents this:

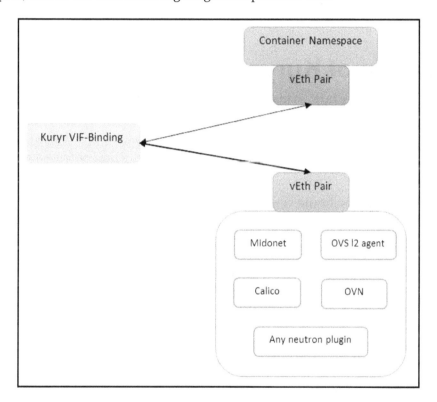

Providing containerized images of neutron plugins

Kuryr aims to provide containerized images of the various neutron plugins that are integrated with Kolla, as well.

Nesting VMs and Magnum use cases

Kuryr addresses Magnum project use cases in terms of container networking and serves as a unified interface for Magnum or any other OpenStack project that needs to leverage container networking through the neutron API. In this regard, Kuryr leverages neutron plugins that support VM nested container use cases and enhances neutron APIs to support these cases (for example, OVN).

Installation of Kuryr

In this section, we will see how to install Kuryr. The prerequisites are as follows:

- KeyStone
- Neutron
- A DB management system such as MySQL or MariaDB (for neutron and KeyStone)
- Neutron agents for the vendor you choose
- Rabbitmq if the neutron agents for your vendor require it
- Docker 1.9+

The following steps run Kuryr inside a Docker container:

1. Pull the upstream Kuryr libnetwork Docker image:

   ```
   $ docker pull kuryr/libnetwork:latest
   ```

2. Prepare Docker to find the Kuryr driver:

   ```
   $ sudo mkdir -p /usr/lib/docker/plugins/kuryr
   $ sudo curl -o /usr/lib/docker/plugins/kuryr/kuryr.spec \
            https://raw.githubusercontent.com/openstack/kuryr-
   libnetwork/master/etc/kuryr.spec
   $ sudo service docker restart
   ```

3. Start the Kuryr container:

   ```
   $ docker run --name kuryr-libnetwork \
   --net=host \
   --cap-add=NET_ADMIN \
   -e SERVICE_USER=admin \;
   -e SERVICE_PROJECT_NAME=admin \
   -e SERVICE_PASSWORD=admin \
   ```

```
-e SERVICE_DOMAIN_NAME=Default \
-e USER_DOMAIN_NAME=Default \
-e IDENTITY_URL=http://127.0.0.1:35357/v3 \
-v /var/log/kuryr:/var/log/kuryr \
-v /var/run/openvswitch:/var/run/openvswitch \
        kuryr/libnetwork
```

Here:

- SERVICE_USER, SERVICE_PROJECT_NAME, SERVICE_PASSWORD, SERVICE_DOMAIN_NAME, and USER_DOMAIN_NAME are OpenStack credentials
- IDENTITY_URL is the URL to the OpenStack KeyStone v3 endpoint
- A volume is created so that the logs are available on the host
- NET_ADMIN capabilities are given in order to perform network operations on the host namespace, such as ovs-vsctl

Walk-through

Kuryr exists in each host that runs containers and serves APIs required for the libnetwork remote network driver.

The following are the steps which are executed to create a container network provided by the neutron:

1. A user sends a request to libnetwork to create a Docker network with the network driver specifier as Kuryr. The following example creates a Docker network named bar:

   ```
   $ sudo docker network create --driver=kuryr --ipam-driver=kuryr --subnet 10.0.0.0/16 --gateway 10.0.0.1 --ip-range 10.0.0.0/24 bar
   ```

2. libnetwork makes API calls to the Kuryr plugin to create the network
3. Kuryr forwards the call to the Neutron and Neutron creates the network with the input data provided by Kuryr
4. Upon receiving a response from the neutron, it prepares the output and sends it to libnetwork
5. libnetwork stores the response to its key/value datastore backend
6. The user can then launch a container using the network created previously:

   ```
   $ sudo docker run --net=bar -itd --name=nginx-container nginx
   ```

Summary

In this chapter, we learned about Kuryr. We learnt what Kuryr is, its architecture, and its installation process. We also looked at the overall workflow when a user creates a Docker network using Kuryr as the network driver.

The next chapter will focus on project Murano. We will learn about Murano and its architecture and complete hands-on exercises.

8
Murano – Containerized Application Deployment on OpenStack

This chapter will explain the OpenStack project, Murano, which is the application catalog to OpenStack that enables application developers and cloud administrators to publish various cloud-ready applications in a browsable categorized catalog. Murano greatly eases the application deployment on the OpenStack infrastructure with just a click. In this chapter, we will discuss the following topics:

- Introduction to Murano
- Murano concepts
- Key features
- Murano components
- Walk-through
- Murano DevStack installation
- Deploying containerized application

Introduction to Murano

Murano is the OpenStack application catalog service, which provides various cloud-ready applications to be easily deployed on OpenStack, abstracting all the complexities behind. It simplifies the packaging and deployment of various applications on top of OpenStack IaaS. It is an integration point for external applications and OpenStack with the support of complete life cycle management of applications. Murano applications can be run inside Docker containers or Kubernetes Pod.

Murano is a powerful solution for end users, looking for application deployment on top of OpenStack, who don't want to worry about deployment complexities.

The following is a list of features provided by Murano:

- Provides production ready applications and dynamic UI
- Supports running containerized application
- Supports provisioning applications on both Windows and Linux systems
- Secures data with Barbican
- Supports running application packages using **Heat Orchestration Templates (HOT)**
- Deploys multiregion application
- Allows attaching of Cinder volumes to the VMs in an application and storing of packages in Glare
- Packages similar packages in a bundle, such as container-based apps
- Provides statistics related to the environment and applications for billing purpose

Murano concepts

In this section, we will discuss the different concepts used in Murano.

Environment

An environment in Murano represents a set of applications, which is managed by a single tenant. No two tenants can share the applications in an environment. Also an application in one environment is independent of other environments. Multiple applications, that are logically related in an environment, can together form a more complex application.

Package

A package in Murano is a ZIP archive that contains all the installation scripts, class definitions, dynamic UI forms, image lists, and the instruction of an application deployment. This package is imported by Murano and used for deploying an application. Various packages can be uploaded to Murano for different applications.

Session

Murano allows modification to an environment from multiple users who are from different locations. To allow modification from multiple users at the same time, Murano uses sessions that stores local modification from all users. A session is created when any application is added to an environment, and after the deployment is started, the session becomes invalid. A session can't be shared among multiple users.

The environment template

A set of applications can form a complex application. To define such applications, Murano uses the concept of **environment template**. Each application in the template is managed by a single tenant. This template can be deployed by translating it into an environment.

Deployments

A deployment is used to represent a process of installing an application. It stores information such as environment status, events, and errors in any application deployment.

Bundle

A bundle in Murano represents a group of similar applications. Applications in a bundle need not to be closely related. They are sorted according to usage.

An example for this is, creating a bundle of database apps consisting of a MySQL or Oracle application. A bundle can be imported directly in Murano, which will in turn import all the applications in the bundle.

Categories

Applications can be grouped into different categories, based on their types, such as application servers, big data, and databases.

Key features

Murano has many advanced features that makes it a strong solution for application management on OpenStack. In this section, we will talk about some of the advanced features in Murano.

Production-ready applications

Murano has various cloud-ready applications that can be configured very easily on either VM or baremetal. This doesn't need any knowledge of installation, infrastructure management, and so on, making deployment of complex applications an easy task for OpenStack users. Users can choose to run their application on Docker Host or Kubernetes Pod.

Application catalog UI

Murano provides a UI for end users to easily browse the applications available. Users can deploy any complex application with just a push of a button. The UI is dynamic, in the sense that it provides forms for user input while an application is provisioned. It also allows application tagging, provides information about each application, shows recent activities, and so on.

Distributing workloads

Murano allows its users to select regions while provisioning any application. This way, your application can be distributed in cross-regions for achieving scalability and high availability while any disaster recovery.

Application development

Murano Programming Language (**MuranoPL**) can be used to define an application. It uses YAML and YAQL for application definition. It also has some core libraries that define the common function used in several applications. MuranoPL also supports garbage collection, which means it deallocates all the resources of an application.

Murano repository

Murano supports installing packages from different sources such as a file, URL, and repository. Murano can import an application package from a custom repository. It downloads all the dependent packages and images, if defined from the repository for application deployment.

 Refer to
https://docs.openstack.org/murano/latest/admin/appdev-guide/mura
nopackages/repository.html for setting up a custom repository.

Cinder volumes

Murano supports the attaching of Cinder volumes to the VMs in an application and also supports the booting of these VMs from a Cinder volume. Multiple volumes can be attached to an application for storage purpose.

 Refer to
https://docs.openstack.org/murano/latest/admin/appdev-guide/cind
er_volume_supporting.html for the detailed step of using Cinder
volumes with Murano.

Barbican support

Barbican is the OpenStack project to support sensitive data such as password and certificates. Murano ensures that your data is secured by storing it in Barbican. You need to install Barbican, and configure Murano to use Barbican as the backend storage solution.

HOT packages

Murano supports the composing of an application package from the Heat template. You can add any Heat template to Murano as a new package for deployment. Murano supports both the automatic and manual way of composing an application package from the Heat template.

 Refer to https://docs.openstack.org/murano/latest/admin/appdev-guide/hot_packages.html for details on using Heat templates with Murano.

Murano components

The figure in *The Murano dashboard* section explains the architecture of Murano. Murano has a similar architecture to other OpenStack components. It also has the API service and an engine as the main components. There are other components as well, such as murano-agent, Murano dashboard, and the python client, that is, murano-pythonclient. Let's take a look at each component in detail.

The Murano API

The Murano API (murano-api) is a WSGI server that serves the API requests of users. The Murano API has different controllers for each resource type. Each controller handles a request for specific resources. They validate the request for permissions, validate the data provided in the request, and create a DB object for the resource with the input data. The request is forwarded to the murano-engine service. Upon receiving a response from murano-engine, the murano-api service returns the response to the user.

The Murano engine

The Murano engine (murano-engine) is the service where most of the orchestration happens. It makes a series of calls to Heat, the OpenStack Orchestration service, to create the infrastructural resources, such as VMs and volumes, required for the deployment of the application. It also starts an agent known as murano-agent inside the VMs, to do the installation of external applications.

The Murano agent

The Murano agent (murano-agent) is a service that runs inside the VMs of a deployment. It does the software configuration and installation on the VMs. VM images are built using this agent.

The Murano dashboard

The Murano dashboard provides the Web UI to the users for easy, browsable access to the application available in Murano. It supports role-based access control for it users:

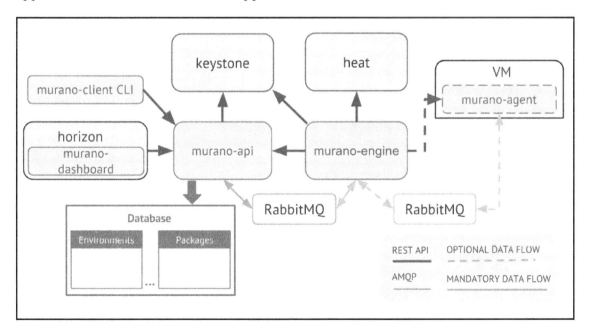

Walk-through

In this section, we will do a walk-through on how an application is deployed by Murano. Murano interacts with multiple OpenStack services for resources needed for application deployment.

The request flow for deploying an application in Murano is as follows:

1. The user sends a REST API call to the `murano-api` service for deploying an environment via a CLI or Horizon when an authentication token is received from KeyStone

2. The `murano-api` service receives the request and sends the request for validation token and access permission to KeyStone

3. KeyStone validates the token and sends updated authentications headers with roles and permissions

4. The `murano-api` service checks whether the session is valid or not. If the session is not valid or already deployed, the request fails with a `403` HTTP status

5. A check is done to check if the environment was deleted previously or not. If not deleted, an entry is made in the task table to store the information of this action

6. The `murano-api` service sends the request to the `murano-engine` service via an RPC asynchronous call with the JSON object containing class types, application details, and the user data, if any

7. The `murano-engine` service picks the request from the message queue

8. It creates a KeyStone trust, which is to be used with the application

9. It downloads the needed packages, and also validates if the required class are available and accessible

10. The `murano-engine` service then creates all the classes defined in the model sent to it

11. Then the deploy method for each application is called. In this stage, `murano-engine` interacts with Heat to create networks, VMs, and other resources needed for the application to run

12. After the instance is running, a userdata script is run to install and run `murano-agent` on the VM

13. The `murano-agent` service does the software configuration and installation steps

14. After the installation is done, `murano-engine` sends a response to the API service about the completion

15. The `murano-api` service then marks the environment as deployed in the database

Murano DevStack installation

We will now see how to install a development setup of Murano using DevStack.

1. Create a root directory for DevStack if needed:

```
$ sudo mkdir -p /opt/stack
$ sudo chown $USER /opt/stack
```

2. Clone DevStack repository:

```
$ git clone https://git.openstack.org/openstack-dev/devstack
/opt/stack/devstack
```

3. Now create a minimal `local.conf` for running the DevStack setup:

```
$ cat > /opt/stack/devstack/local.conf << END
[[local|localrc]]
HOST_IP=$(ip addr | grep 'state UP' -A2 | tail -n1 | awk '{print
$2}' | cut -f1  -d'/')
DATABASE_PASSWORD=password
RABBIT_PASSWORD=password
SERVICE_TOKEN=password
SERVICE_PASSWORD=password
ADMIN_PASSWORD=password
enable_plugin murano git://git.openstack.org/openstack/murano
END
```

4. Now run DevStack:

```
$ cd /opt/stack/devstack
$ ./stack.sh
```

Murano should be installed now. To verify the installation, run the following:

```
$ sudo systemctl status devstack@murano-*
  devstack@murano-engine.service - Devstack devstack@murano-
engine.service
   Loaded: loaded (/etc/systemd/system/devstack@murano-
engine.service; enabled; vendor preset: enabled)
   Active: active (running) since Thu 2017-11-02 04:32:28 EDT; 2
weeks 5 days ago
 Main PID: 30790 (murano-engine)
   CGroup: /system.slice/system-devstack.slice/devstack@murano-
engine.service
           ├─30790 /usr/bin/python /usr/local/bin/murano-engine --
config-file /etc/murano/murano.conf
           ├─31016 /usr/bin/python /usr/local/bin/murano-engine --
config-file /etc/murano/murano.conf
           ├─31017 /usr/bin/python /usr/local/bin/murano-engine --
config-file /etc/murano/murano.conf
           ├─31018 /usr/bin/python /usr/local/bin/murano-engine --
config-file /etc/murano/murano.conf
           └─31019 /usr/bin/python /usr/local/bin/murano-engine --
config-file /etc/murano/murano.conf
  devstack@murano-api.service - Devstack devstack@murano-api.service
   Loaded: loaded (/etc/systemd/system/devstack@murano-api.service;
enabled; vendor preset: enabled)
   Active: active (running) since Thu 2017-11-02 04:32:26 EDT; 2
weeks 5 days ago
 Main PID: 30031 (uwsgi)
   Status: "uWSGI is ready"
   CGroup: /system.slice/system-devstack.slice/devstack@murano-
api.service
           ├─30031 /usr/local/bin/uwsgi --ini /etc/murano/murano-api-
uwsgi.ini
           ├─30034 /usr/local/bin/uwsgi --ini /etc/murano/murano-api-
uwsgi.ini
           └─30035 /usr/local/bin/uwsgi --ini /etc/murano/murano-api-
uwsgi.ini
```

You can see that both the `murano-api` and `murano-engine` services are up and running.

Deploying a containerized application

In the previous section, you learned how to install Murano with DevStack. Now we will see how to use Murano in order to install an application on OpenStack. As Murano is all about the ease that it provides with the browsable, dynamic UI, we will use the **Application Catalog** tab in Horizon to run our application.

We will install an NGINX containerized application inside Docker in this example. We will need the following packages for running this application:

- **Docker Interface Library**: This library defines a framework for building Docker applications. It provides the data structures and common interfaces used by all the applications and hosting services backed by Docker.
- **Docker Standalone Host**: This is a regular Docker host application. All the container applications are run inside a dedicated VM running image built with Docker and `murano-agent`.
- **Kubernetes Pod**: This application provides an infrastructure for running containerized applications with Kubernetes. Kubernetes is installed on OpenStack VMs. This is optional for the **Docker Standalone Host** application.
- **Nginx applications**: Nginx is a web server application that will be run using either **Docker Standalone Host** or **Kubernetes Pod** application.

All the container applications for Murano can be found at `https://github.com/openstack/k8s-docker-suite-app-murano`.

Now let's start using the Murano dashboard to run our container application. Log in to your Horizon dashboard by entering your credentials:

1. Download the packages from `https://github.com/openstack/k8s-docker-suite-app-murano`
2. Create a `.zip` archive for each of the preceding listed applications
3. Now navigate to **App Catalogue** | **Manage** | **Packages** on the dashboard
4. Click on **Import Package**

Select **File** as **Package Source**, and browse to upload the ZIP file of your application. Fill in the UI form with necessary details for each application and click on **Click** to finish uploading a package. You can now browse the available application by navigating to **App Catalogue** | **Browse** | **Browse Local**. You will see a page like this:

5. Build the VM image by following the steps provided at `https://github.com/ openstack/k8s-docker-suite-app-murano/tree/master/ DockerStandaloneHost/elements`

6. Mark the image to be used by Murano. Navigate to **App Catalogue** | **Manage** | **Marked Images**, click on **Mark Image**, and fill the details exactly as provided in the following screenshot:

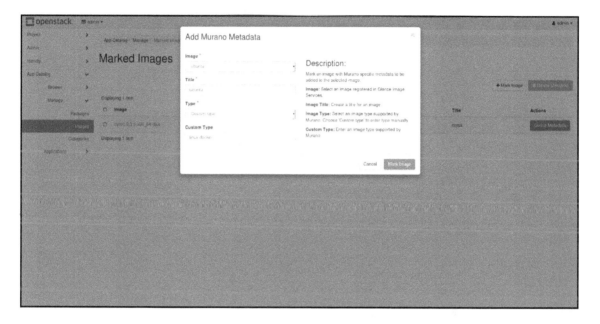

7. Deploy an application by clicking on **Quick Deploy**

You can see in the following screenshot that we are given two options to choose for our container host: **Kubernetes Pod** and **Docker Standalone Host**. We will choose the latter one as the option:

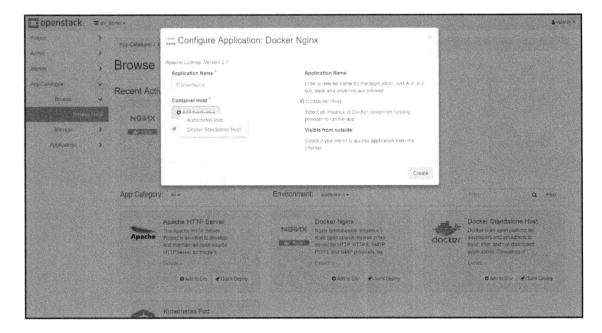

8. Fill in the details for the VM to be created for running our application, as shown here:

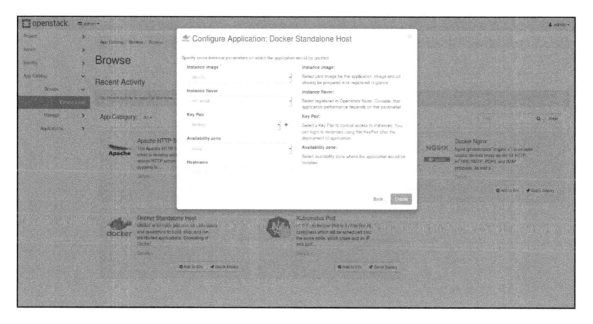

9. Click on **Create** to create the environment for our deployment

You will be automatically redirected to the newly created environment in **App Catalogue** | **Applications** | **Environment**.

10. Click on **Deploy Environment** to start the installation of your application and the necessary infrastructure required.

You will see the following screenshot, which shows that it started creating the VM on which Docker will run:

Upon the successful completion of the preceding deployment, you will be able to see that a new VM will be created, as shown in the following screenshot, and your Nginx application running in a Docker container inside the VM:

You can log in to the VM and access the Nginx application. We have now successfully installed a containerized Nginx application on OpenStack.

Summary

In this chapter, you learned about Murano, which is the application catalog service for OpenStack, in detail. We looked into the different concepts available in Murano. Then, you also learned about the components and architecture of Murano. The chapter also gave a detailed overview of the workflow of a user request for deploying an application with Murano. Then we saw how to install a development setup of Murano using DevStack, and we did a hands-on on using the Murano dashboard to create an environment, add applications to it, and deploy the environment.

In the next chapter, you will learn about Kolla, which provides production ready containers and tools for deployment of the OpenStack services.

9
Kolla – Containerized Deployment of OpenStack

In this chapter, you will learn about Kolla. It provides production-ready containers and deployment tools for operating OpenStack cloud. The contents of this chapter are as follows:

- Kolla introduction
- Key features
- Architecture
- Deploying containerized OpenStack services

Kolla introduction

The OpenStack cloud consists of multiple services, and each service interacts with other services. There is no integrated product release for OpenStack. Each project follows a release cycle after every 6 months. This provides a greater flexibility for operators to choose from multiple options and builds a custom deployment solution for them. However, this also brings a complexity of deploying and managing the OpenStack cloud.

There is need for these services to be scalable, upgradable, and readily available. Kolla provides a way for running these services inside containers, and this adds the advantage to the OpenStack cloud being fast, reliable, scalable, and upgradeable. Kolla packs the OpenStack services and their requirements, and sets up all the configuration in the container images.

Kolla uses Ansible to run these container images and deploy or upgrade OpenStack cluster very easily on bare metal or VMs. Kolla containers are configured to store the data on persistent storage, which can then be mounted back onto the host operating system and restored successfully to protect against any faults.

In order to deploy OpenStack, Kolla has three projects as follows:

- **kolla:** All the Docker container images for OpenStack projects are maintained in this project. Kolla provides an image building tool called kolla-build to build container images for most of the projects.
- **kolla-ansible**: This provides Ansible playbooks for deploying OpenStack inside Docker containers. It supports both the all-in-one and multi-node setups of the OpenStack cloud.
- **kolla-kubernetes**: This deploys OpenStack on Kubernetes. This aims to leverage the self-healing, health checks, upgrade, and other capabilities of Kubernetes for managing containerized OpenStack deployment. kolla-kubernetes uses Ansible playbooks and the Jinja2 template to generate configuration files for the services.

Key features

In this section, we will see some of the key features of Kolla.

Highly available deployment

The OpenStack ecosystem consists of multiple services running only a single instance of them, which sometimes becomes the single point of failure in case of any disaster, and it can't scale beyond a single instance. To make it scalable, Kolla deploys the OpenStack cloud, configured with HA. So even if any service fails, it can scale without any interruption to the current operations. This feature makes Kolla an ideal solution for easy upgrade and scale without any downtime.

Ceph support

Kolla uses Ceph to add persistent data to the VMs running our OpenStack environment, so that we can easily recover from any disaster, hence making the OpenStack cloud more reliable. Ceph is also used for storing glance images.

Image building

Kolla provides a tool called kolla-build to build container images on multiple distros such as CentOs, Ubuntu, Debian, and Oracle Linux. Multiple dependent components can be built at once.

Docker hub support

You can pull images from Docker Hub directly. You can see all the Kolla images at `https://hub.docker.com/u/kolla/`.

Local registry support

Kolla also supports pushing images to the local registry. Refer to `https://docs.openstack.org/kolla-ansible/latest/user/multinode.html#deploy-a-registry` for setting a local registry.

Multiple build sources

Kolla supports building from multiple sources binary and source. The binaries are the packages installed by the package manager of the host OS, whereas the source could be a URL, local repository, or tarball. Refer to `https://docs.openstack.org/kolla/latest/admin/image-building.html#build-openstack-from-source` for more details.

Dockerfile customization

Kolla supports building images from Jinja2 templates, which provide a better flexibility for customization by operators. Operators can customize their image building to include additional packages, install plugins, change some configuration settings, and so on. Refer to `https://docs.openstack.org/kolla/latest/admin/image-building.html#dockerfile-customisation` for more details on how different customizations can be done.

Architecture

In this section, we will see the OpenStack architecture using Kolla. The following figure shows a **highly available** (**HA**) OpenStack multimode setup done by Kolla.

The infrastructure engineering here means the code or application written for infrastructure management. The code is submitted to Gerrit for review and then the CI system reviews and checks for correctness of the code. Once the code is approved by CI, the CD system feeds the output of build, that is the OpenStack containers that are based on Kolla, into a local registry.

After this, the Ansible contacts Docker and launches our OpenStack multinode environment with HA:

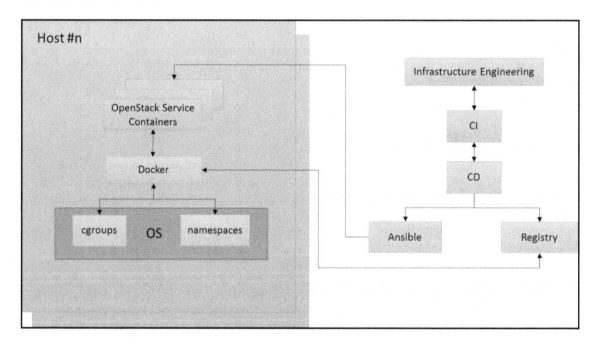

Deploying containerized OpenStack services

In this section, we will understand how Kolla deploys containerized OpenStack using kolla-ansible. At the time of writing, kolla-kubernetes is under development.

Note that this is not a complete guide to Kolla.

Kolla is evolving now, so the guide is upgraded very frequently. Refer to the latest documentation provided at `https://docs.openstack.org/kolla-ansible/latest/`. We will try to explain the general deploy process of OpenStack using Kolla and the subprojects.

Deploying OpenStack with Kolla is pretty easy. Kolla provides both all-in-one and multinode installations on Docker or Kubernetes. It basically involves four steps:

- Setting up a local registry
- Automatic host bootstrap
- Building images
- Deploying images

Setting up a local registry

A local registry is required for storing the container images built by Kolla. It is optional for the all-in-one deployment, the Docker cache can be used instead. Docker Hub contains all the images for all major releases of Kolla. However, it is strongly recommended for the multinode deployment to ensure a single source of images. It is also recommended that you run the registry over HTTPS to secure the images in the production environment.

Refer to the guide at
`https://docs.openstack.org/kolla-ansible/latest/user/multinode.html#deploy-a-registry` for detailed steps for setting up a local registry.

Automatic host bootstrap

Kolla installation requires some packages and tools, such as Docker, libvirt, and NTP, to be installed on the host where we want our OpenStack to run. These dependencies can be automatically installed and configured by host bootstrap. kolla-ansible provides the bootstrap-servers playbook for preparing and installing the hosts for OpenStack installation.

To quickly prepare the host, run this command:

```
$ kolla-ansible -i <inventory_file> bootstrap-servers
```

Building images

In this step, we will build the Docker container images for all OpenStack services. We can specify the base distro for our images, sources, and tags while building the images. The images are pushed to local registry.

Building images in Kolla is as simple as running this command:

```
$ kolla-build
```

This command by default builds all the images based on CentOS. To build images with a specific distro, use the -b option:

```
$ kolla-build -b ubuntu
```

To build images for a specific project, pass the name of the project to the command:

```
$ kolla-build nova zun
```

One advanced feature in Kolla is the image profiles. Profiles are used to define a set of related projects in OpenStack. Some of the defined profiles in Kolla are as follows:

- **infra**: All infra-related projects
- **main**: These are the OpenStack core projects such as Nova, Neutron, KeyStone, and Horizon
- **aux**: These are the additional projects such as Zun and Ironic
- **default**: These are a set of minimum projects required for a ready cloud

New profiles can be defined in the `kolla-build.conf` object as well. To do this, just add a new profile under the `[profile]` section in the `.conf` file:

```
[profiles]
containers=zun,magnum,heat
```

In the preceding example, we set a new profile called `containers` to represent a group of projects related to containerization in OpenStack. The `heat` project is also mentioned and used because it is required by `magnum`. Also, you can use this profile to create images for these projects:

```
$ kolla-build -profile containers
```

Images can also be pushed to Docker Hub or to the local registry using these commands:

```
$ kolla-build -push # push to Docker Hub
$ kolla-build -registry <URL> --push # push to local registry
```

> Kolla also provides more advanced operations such as building image from source and Docker file customization. You can refer to
> https://docs.openstack.org/kolla/latest/admin/image-building.htm
> l for more details.

Deploying images

Now we have all the images required for OpenStack deployment; kolla-ansible contacts Docker and provides these images for running them. The deployment can be all-in-one or mutlinode. The decision is made on the Ansible inventory files available in kolla-ansible. This inventory file contains the information about the infrastructure hosts in the cluster. The deploy process in Kolla takes the environment variables and passwords specified in the configuration files and an inventory file to provision the highly available OpenStack cluster.

All the configuration options and passwords used for OpenStack deployment are stored in `/etc/kolla/globals.yml` and `/etc/kolla/passwords.yml`, respectively. Edit these files manually to specify your choice of installation, as shown here:

```
kolla_base_distro: "centos"
kolla_install_type: "source"
```

You can generate a password with this command:

```
$ kolla-genpwd
```

You can run `prechecks` on the deployment targets nodes to check whether they are in the state or not:

```
$ kolla-ansible prechecks -i <inventory-file>
```

Now we are ready to deploy OpenStack. Run the following command:

```
$ kolla-ansible deploy -i <inventory-file>
```

To verify the installation, see the containers list in `docker`:

```
$ docker ps -a
```

You should see all the OpenStack service containers running. Now let's generate the `admin-openrc.sh` file to use our OpenStack cluster. The generated file will be stored in the `/etc/kolla` directory:

```
$ kolla-ansible post-deploy
```

Now install `python-openstackclient`:

```
$ pip install python-openstackclient
```

To initialize the neutron networks and glance image, run this command:

```
$ . /etc/kolla/admin-openrc.sh
#On centOS
$ /usr/share/kolla-ansible/init-runonce
#ubuntu
$ /usr/local/share/kolla-ansible/init-runonce
```

After the successful deployment of OpenStack, you can access the Horizon dashboard. Horizon will be available at the IP address or hostname specified in `kolla_external_fqdn`, or `kolla_internal_fqdn`. If these variables were not set during deployment, they default to `kolla_internal_vip_address`.

Refer to
`https://docs.openstack.org/project-deploy-guide/kolla-ansible/la test/multinode.html` for detailed steps of deploying a multi-node OpenStack cloud using kolla-ansible and `https://docs.openstack.org/ kolla-kubernetes/latest/deployment-guide.html` using kolla-kubernetes.

Summary

In this chapter, you learned about Kolla, which deploys a containerized OpenStack cloud. We looked at various projects available in Kolla and learned what they do in general. Then we looked into some of the key features of Kolla and discussed the Kolla architecture for OpenStack deployment. You also learned how to build images with Kolla and finally understand the deployment process of Kolla.

In the next chapter, we will look at the best practices for securing your containers and also the advantages of using different OpenStack projects.

10
Best Practices for Containers and OpenStack

In this chapter, we will focus on the advantages of running your containers on OpenStack and best practices for deploying and securing your containers on OpenStack. Specifically, we will look at the following topics:

- The advantages of different OpenStack projects
- Best practices for securing and deploying containers

The advantages of different OpenStack projects

OpenStack provides the resources and services that container platforms and applications can use. It provides standards for building scalable clouds. It also provides shared networking, storage, and many other advanced services. It has programmable APIs, which can be used to create the infrastructure on demand. Users can use different OpenStack services for their container-related workloads.

Users can use Magnum to provision and manage their COEs. Magnum provides the multitenant capability, which means that one COE cluster belongs to only one tenant. This enables container isolation, and containers belonging to different tenants are not scheduled on the same hosts. Magnum has built-in support for Kubernetes, Swarm, and Mesos. Magnum also provides TLS support to secure communication between the services of a cluster and the outside world.

Users can use Zun to deploy their container workloads directly to OpenStack without using COEs. Zun provides full container life cycle management support. It also provides Docker networking support via Kuryr. This means that users can use Neutron networking for their container and virtual machine workloads, and access each other from inside them. Zun also provides OpenStack Cinder support for persistent storage in containers. Zun has built-in multitenant capabilities and authentication support using KeyStone.

OpenStack Kolla provides support to deploy OpenStack services insides containers. It results in new, fast, reliable, and composable building blocks. Kolla simplifies deployment and ongoing operations by packaging each service, for the most part, as a microservice in a Docker container. Users can use Kolla to deploy OpenStack services in Docker containers or Kubernetes pods.

For deploying their containerized application on OpenStack, users can use Murano. Murano will create the infrastructure for deployment and deploy the containerized applications on them.

Best practices for securing and deploying containers

Containers are replacing virtual machines for running most of the enterprise software due to their modularity and portability between servers. However, there are some risks associated with containers. One obvious risk is related to distributing containers by cloning them as images. If there is any unpatched vulnerability in a base image, all clones and applications inheriting from the base image will suffer too.

The second and major risk is the default user of the container systems, that is, the root user. If an attacker gains access to a root user, which allows an escape from the container, he can get access to not only inside the other containers, but also to the root privileges in the host operating system. And it can be devastating!

Here are some best practices for securing and deploying containers:

- Users should always use a lightweight Linux operating system. A lightweight operating system, reduces the chances of attack. It also makes applying the updates a lot easier.
- Users should keep all container images updated. Keeping all images updated ensures that they are free from the latest vulnerabilities. Always keep your images in centralized repositories by versioning and tagging them.

- Users should automate all security updates. This ensures that patches are applied quickly to your infrastructure.
- Users should always scan their container images for potential defects. There are many scanning tools, such as Clair by CoreOS, Dockscan, and Twistlock, which compare container manifests with lists of known vulnerabilities and alert you when they detect any vulnerability.
- Users should not run extraneous network-facing services in containers.
- Users should avoid mounting a host directory inside containers, because it may give access to some sensitive data on hosts inside containers.
- Users should always define restrictions on the resource consumption of containers. It will help to avoid the consumption of all the resources on the host and starving other containers.
- Users should secure their Docker hosts, and they should not provide sensitive information such as the root user's credentials to other users.
- Users should run their Docker registry using TLS. Only valid users should be able to pull and push images to the registry.
- Users should always monitor the container behaviors for anomalies.
- Users can use clear containers or open source Hyper for more security because they provide more isolation.

Summary

Throughout this book, we came across several container-related projects in OpenStack and their key features. In this chapter, we summarized the advantages of all the projects explained in the book for running your container workloads. We also explained different security issues in containers and best practices to resolve them.

Index

F

features, Kolla
  about 142
  Ceph support 142
  Docker hub support 143
  Dockerfile, customization 143
  highly available deployment 142
  local registry support 143
  multiple build sources 143
features, Magnum
  about 83
  container, monitoring 85, 86
  Kubernetes, external load balancer 83
  notifications 85
  scaling 84
  storage 84
  TLS 83, 84
features, Murano
  about 126
  application Catalog UI 126
  application development 127
  Barbican support 128
  Cinder volumes 127
  distributing workloads 127
  HOT packages 128
  production ready applications 126
  repository 127
features, Zun
  about 102
  Cinder integration 103
  container, creating 103
  CPU sets 103, 104
  Kuryr networking 103
  sandbox container 103
Fuxi 78

G

generic VIF-Binding infrastructure
  providing 119
Glance
  about 61
  database 61
  glance-api 61
  glance-registry 61

H

Heat 77
Heat Orchestration Templates (HOT) 124
Heat Stack Template (HOT) 81
highly available (HA) 144
HOT packages
  about 128
  reference link 128
Hyper-V containers 16
Hyper-V virtual machines 16

I

identity service 55
image drivers 102
image service
  about 61
  metadata definition service 61
  storage repository 61
Infrastructure as a Service (IaaS) 76

K

Kernel namespaces 11
KeyStone 55
KeyStone user
  creating 67
Kolla
  about 77, 141
  reference link 145, 147
  references 148
  using, for OpenStack architecture 144
Kubernetes architecture
  about 34
  external request 35
  master node 35
  worker nodes 36
Kubernetes
  about 34
  concepts 37
  deployments 38
  examples 45, 52
  external load balancer 83
  installing 39, 40, 41, 43, 45
  labels 38
  pod 37

www.ingramcontent.com/pod-product-compliance
Lightning Source LLC
Chambersburg PA
CBHW080532060326
40690CB00022B/5098